The Sacred Person

A Theological and Apologetic Examination

by

Dr. ant

The Sacred Person: A Theological and Apologetic Examination

The Sacred Person: A Theological and Apologetic Examination

Contents

Introduction

In the grand tapestry of human existence, where each thread bears the weight of choice, belief, and consequence, the notion of human dignity stands as a keystone. The heart of our discourse orbits this fundamental premise: that every human being, endowed by Divine Providence, holds within an irreplaceable sanctity. It is this sanctity that the Church has long championed, often against the turbulent gales of worldly dissent and misunderstanding.

The term "human dignity" reverberates through the annals of history, echoing from the Psalms of King David to the encyclicals of modern Popes. It is not merely a transient or ornamental concept but a timeless truth, bridging the sacred and the secular, the ancient and the contemporary. In this treatise, we endeavor to traverse these grand vistas, shedding light upon the pillars upon which the dignity of the human person rests. We invite theologians to enliven their spirit, sociologists to sharpen their inquiry, and Catholics to reaffirm their trust in the Church's moral compass.

Let us ascend, then, to our first summit—the Scriptural basis for human dignity. Sacred Scriptures, in their wisdom and veneration, sing in harmonious accord the value of the human person. From the Genesis narrative declaring mankind's creation in the imago Dei to the New Testament's affirmation that each individual is a temple of the Holy Spirit, the Biblical tradition serves as our earliest instructor. By dissecting both Old and New Testament teachings, we unearth a foundation of unshakable worth and intrinsic value, intertwining our divine likeness with earthly sojourn.

Pivoting from the Scriptural to the theological, the legacy left by the Church Fathers augments our understanding. Augustine, whose penetrating intellect and profound spirituality shaped Christian thought, viewed human nature through the lens of both grace and fallenness. His contemplations on the human condition echo in the corridors of theological discourse, urging us to reconcile our imperfections with our created glory. Then comes Aquinas, whose synthesis of Aristotelian insight and Christian doctrine yielded a comprehensive philosophy of the sacred person. His is not merely theology but a symphony merging reason with faith, affirming human dignity with unprecedented clarity and rigor.

Yet, the story of human dignity cannot be confined to ancient texts alone. We must account for the currents of time and thought that shaped modern theological landscapes. The convocations of the Second Vatican Council unveiled new dimensions of human personhood, addressing both the spiritual and existential crises of contemporary society. This fresh breath of ecclesiastical life beckons us to revisit our notions of dignity, making them relevant in an ever-evolving world.

Philosophy, too, has lent its voice to our chorus, providing secular underpinnings that resonate with theological affirmations. Aristotle's profound deliberations on human nature offer invaluable insights, ingraining ethical and logical coherence into our understanding of dignity. The stoic traditions, with their emphasis on inner virtue and moral fortitude, champion the dignity intrinsic to the rational agent. Such perspectives, though divergent in origin, converge upon a fundamental appreciation for human worth, stitching philosophical tapestries that complement our religious convictions.

A balanced evaluation of moral teachings within the Church reveals doctrinal bedrocks, such as the Ten Commandments and the Catechism, which guide the believer's conduct. Far from being mere edicts, these moral teachings serve as pathways to a life infused with virtue and integrity, upholding human dignity against the encroachments of moral relativism and ethical ambiguity.

Our defense of human dignity does not solely reside in rational and theological argument but blossoms in apologetics. Among the tools of rational defense, logical reasoning lays bare the arguments supporting human worth and systematically counters objections that seek to undermine it. Scriptural apologetics, rich in Biblical evidence, fortifies our standpoint, addressing common contentions with the wisdom of centuries.

In addressing the relationship between dignity and life, we scrutinize the ethical dimensions underscored by the Church's teachings on abortion, euthanasia, and the sanctity of life. These are not mere ideological stances, but profound affirmations of the inviolability of life in all its stages—from the unborn and the infirm to the elderly and the marginalized. Each stage of life, in its vulnerability and potential, demands our protection and our veneration.

The mission towards social justice within the Church framework elucidates the principles of Catholic Social Teaching. This mission reaffirms our commitment to the preferential option for the poor, urging solidarity and subsidiarity within the societal lattice. The Church's role in social justice extends beyond pulpit proclamations to concrete actions, demonstrated through historical context and modern applications, and through poignant case studies of advocacy and reform.

We also confront the ever-pertinent matter of the conscience in moral decision-making. Exploring the nature of conscience, its formation, and the indispensable role of grace and free will, we prepare ourselves for the moral choices of everyday life. Here we delve into personal and complex ethical dilemmas, seeking light from Church guidance to navigate the moral intricacies of existence.

The Church, in its vast wisdom, addresses human rights with deep theological resonance. By delving into core documents and declarations, we align and scrutinize secular and sacred rights. This alignment, however, is not without its conflicts and challenges, necessitating diligent resolution and practical solutions to bridge these spheres.

Emerging scientific discoveries challenge and enrich the discourse on human dignity. The Church's response to advances in medical science, genetic engineering, and emerging technologies compels a balance between faith and reason. Through ethical guidelines and a profound respect for human uniqueness, we chart a course that honors both scientific inquiry and theological integrity.

Each individual's personal vocation, a calling to holiness and discernment, positions the concept of dignity within the personal journey. By understanding vocation, we can perceive how lives interweave with family, community, and the saintly exemplars who guide us on our path. Living out one's vocation, thus, becomes an imperative expression of human dignity.

Anticipating the future, we acknowledge the modern world's challenges—increasing secularism and complex global ethical considerations. The Church's role in forthcoming advocacy, through initiatives for education and creating a culture of respect, charts a hopeful trajectory for the impregnable dignity of the human person.

In this sacred endeavor, we bind together threads ancient and new, rational and divine, individual and collective. The defense and celebration of human dignity is not mere philosophy or dry doctrine, but a living testimony to the grandeur of the human spirit, fashioned in the likeness of the Creator and destined for eternal glory.

Chapter 1: The Foundations of Human Dignity

The essence of human dignity, an unassailable tenet etched within the heart of Holy Scripture, reverberates through the Old and New Testaments, embracing the unparalleled worth of each person. From the genesis of humankind fashioned from dust and divine breath, to the New Covenant's affirmation of eternal value in Christ, the sacred texts render a tapestry rich with the innate sanctity of the human condition. This primordial respect for man and woman surpasses mere existence, pointing to an existential grandeur bestowed by the Creator Himself. Hence, the Church's moral teachings do not merely instruct; they exalt, preserving a cosmic recognition that humanity, in its frailty and strength, is the handiwork of God, crowned in dignity and purpose unparalleled.

Scriptural Basis for Human Dignity

The sacred scriptures serve as a foundational bedrock for the exalted value of the human person, illuminating the inherent dignity imbued within us by our Creator. From the dawn of Genesis, where humankind is fashioned in the imago Dei, or the image of God, to the profound declarations of the Psalms, celebrating the fearfully and wonderfully made nature of man, the Old Testament underscores our divine likeness. The New Testament continues this thread, with Christ's Incarnation epitomizing the ultimate affirmation of human worth. The very act of God becoming man confers an unparalleled sanctity upon human existence, marking each individual as a vessel of divine love and a reflection of eternal worth. Thus, Scripture, in its divine narrative, weaves a tapestry rich with the sanctification and exaltation of human dignity, an unerring testament to our sacred value and moral responsibility.

Old Testament Teachings on the Human Person within the grand narrative of the Old Testament, the manifold dimensions of human dignity are profoundly embedded. The Scriptures unveil a panoramic vista, depicting mankind not as mere mortals, but as the very image-bearers of the Divine. From the genesis of creation's tale, one witnesses the inception of human worth in the very breath of God, as He animates the lifeless form of Adam.

In the opening chapters of Genesis, the human person is portrayed with unparalleled significance. "Then God said, 'Let us make man in our image, after our likeness...'" (Gen 1:26). This proclamation is neither a casual utterance nor an afterthought, but a deliberate divine decree. The imago Dei, or the image of God, endows each individual with inherent dignity, setting humankind apart from the rest of creation. The term "image" connotes resemblance and a unique relationship with the Creator, reflecting God's attributes, albeit in limited form.

This ontological foundation is reiterated in the narrative of the fall, demonstrating that even in the state of sin, the essence of human dignity remains untouched. While man may mar his relationship with God, the imago Dei persists. It is this unyielding essence that anchors the idea of redemption later explored in the prophetic writings and fulfilled in the New Testament.

Moreover, the Old Testament constantly alludes to the sanctity and worth of human life through its laws and precepts. The Decalogue, or Ten Commandments, stands as a testament to this principle. "Thou shalt not kill" (Exodus 20:13), a concise yet profound command, underscores the irreplaceable value of human life. This edict is not merely a prohibition but a divine safeguard preserving the sacredness of personhood.

The Hebrew Scriptures further reflect the collective aspect of human dignity. The covenantal relationship between God and Israel portrays a divine commitment to humanity. Through His covenants with patriarchs like Abraham, Moses, and the Davidic line, God reveals that dignity is not solely an individual attribute but encompasses familial, tribal, and national dimensions. The blessings bestowed upon Israel signify a communal identity rooted in divine favor.

Psalms and Proverbs, books of poetic and wisdom literature, offer additional facets of Old Testament teachings on human dignity. The Psalms celebrate human existence as fearfully and wonderfully made, a testament of divine craftsmanship. "For thou hast made him a little lower than the angels, and hast crowned him with glory and honour" (Psalm 8:5). This poetic assertion elevates the human person, affirming the honor bestowed upon each life by the Creator.

In the realm of wisdom literature, the Proverbs impart practical and ethical wisdom, accentuating the just and righteous treatment of others—an acknowledgment of their intrinsic value. "He who oppresses the poor reproaches his Maker, but he who honors Him has mercy on the needy" (Proverbs 14:31). The imperative to honor and respect others, especially the marginalized, points back to the foundational tenet that all are valued in God's sight.

The prophetic literature, replete with calls to justice and righteousness, also aligns with the theme of human dignity. Prophets like Isaiah, Jeremiah, and Amos vehemently advocate for the oppressed and marginalized, underscoring a divine mandate to uphold the dignity of every person. Isaiah eloquently voices God's reassurance: "Fear not, for I have redeemed thee, I have called thee by thy name; thou art mine" (Isaiah 43:1). This divine claim signifies an unbreakable bond and a profound acknowledgment of human worth.

Thus, the Old Testament provides an intricate tapestry that weaves together various threads of human dignity. It portrays individuals as image-bearers of God, upholds the sanctity of life through divine laws, recognizes the communal aspect of dignity in covenant relationships, celebrates human creation in its poetic compositions, and advocates for justice in prophetic exhortations.

In summation, the teachings of the Old Testament present a holistic vision of the human person, imbued with dignity by virtue of divine creation and sustained through covenantal love and justice. This sacred text forms a foundational pillar upon which the subsequent theological reflections in the New Testament will build, collectively affirming the enduring worth and dignity of every human being.

New Testament Affirmations of Human Worth are an irrefutable pillar upon which the edifice of human dignity is constructed. The New Testament, through the missions of Christ and the Apostles, delineates the intrinsic worth of each person, thus fortifying the theological cornerstone set forth in earlier scriptures. As one peruses the annals of the New Testament, it becomes unequivocally clear that every human soul is of inestimable value in the eyes of the Divine.

In the Gospel according to Matthew, we find the Beatitudes, which proclaim the blessedness of the humble, the mournful, and the meek. Here, Christ, in His Sermon on the Mount, recognizeth the dignity of the oppressed and downtrodden. "Blessed are the poor in spirit, for theirs is the kingdom of heaven" (Matthew 5:3). This pronouncement exalts not just the spiritually impoverished but extends the promise of divine filiation to all facets of human suffering and humility, thereby underscoring the sanctity inherent in every human condition.

Moreover, the narrative of the Good Samaritan, detailed in the Gospel of Luke, enjoins us to acknowledge the universal call to compassion. This parable doth illustrate that dignity is not confined to the righteous or the devout but is an attribute bestowed upon every individual by merit of their humanity. When Jesus recounteth the actions of the Samaritan who aids his wounded neighbor, He is compelling His followers to recognize and honor the sacred worth of each person, regardless of societal divisions or prejudices.

In addition, Paul the Apostle's Epistles resound with affirmations of human worth. In his first letter to the Corinthians, Paul declares, "Do you not know that you are God's temple and that God's Spirit dwells in you?" (1 Corinthians 3:16). This assertion not only imbueth believers with a deep sense of spiritual importance but extendeth a profound respect for the human body and soul as vessels of the divine presence. Paul's letters serve as potent reminders of the elevated status humanity holds in the divine schema.

Furthermore, the Epistle to the Galatians underscores the universality of human dignity through its proclamation of equality before God. "There is neither Jew nor Gentile, neither slave nor free, nor is there male and female, for you are all one in Christ Jesus" (Galatians 3:28). This declaration obliterates the barriers of race, class, and gender, affirming the equal worth of every individual, without exception. The theological implications of this are far-reaching, propelling the Church towards a mission of inclusiveness and universal respect.

Consider, too, the Book of Revelation, in which the vision of a new heaven and a new earth transcendeth the temporal limitations of human existence. The imagery employed in Revelation speaks to the ultimate glorification and restoration of humanity, a testament to the perpetual dignity that the faithful are destined to attain. The portrayal of the heavenly Jerusalem is not solely a promise of spiritual utopia but a powerful affirmation of the perpetual worth of those who strive to uphold their sacred dignity on earth.

Let us also not overlook the profound encounter between Christ and the Samaritan woman at the well, as recounted in the Gospel of John. Here, Jesus breaks with societal conventions and bestows upon the woman a recognition of her inherent worth regardless of her social standing or gender. "Whoever drinks the water I give them will never thirst" (John 4:14). This encounter illustrateth not only the transformative power of divine grace but also the irrevocable dignity conferred upon each individual by God's unconditional love and mercy.

The New Testament teachings found in the Acts of the Apostles further corroborate the sanctity and worth of all human beings. Peter's vision at Joppa, where he seeth a large sheet descending from heaven filled with all kinds of animals, and the voice commanding, "Do not call anything impure that God has made clean" (Acts 10:15), reiterateth the theme of universal sanctity. This vision, followed by the conversion of Cornelius the Centurion, underscores the inclusivity of the Christian message and the inherent dignity of all human beings as part of God's creation.

Finally, let us contemplate the sacrificial act of Christ's crucifixion and resurrection. The passion, death, and resurrection of Jesus are not merely central tenets of Christian faith but the ultimate affirmation of human worth. By assuming human nature and sacrificing Himself for the salvation of humanity, Christ elevateth human dignity to a divine plane. "For God so loved the world that He gave His one and only Son, that whoever believes in Him shall not perish but have eternal life" (John 3:16). This supreme act of love and sacrifice enshrineth the immense value of human life and the lengths to which the Divine will go to redeem it.

In summation, the New Testament is replete with affirmations of human worth. From the Gospels to the Epistles to Revelation, the scriptures are imbued with a reverence for the inherent dignity bestowed upon all of humanity. This unassailable truth calls upon the Church and its followers to uphold and defend the sanctity of human life in all its manifestations. The words resonate across the ages, a clarion call to recognize the divine image in each person, and a compelling mandate to honor, protect, and celebrate the incomparable worth of every human soul.

Chapter 2: Theological Perspectives on Human Dignity

In contemplating the essence of human dignity through the lens of theological discourse, one must ponder the august proclamations of the Church Fathers alongside the measured reflections of contemporary theologians. Augustine and Aquinas bequeathed to us a rich heritage, viewing mankind as imago Dei, a sacred reflection of the divine. Such perspectives burgeon in modernity, gaining clarity and fortitude through the declarations of Vatican II, which resound with a clarion call affirming the inestimable worth of the human person. The theological fabric of human dignity is thus interwoven with both the hallowed traditions of antiquity and the evolving interpretations of modern ecclesiastical thought, creating a tapestry that unfurls the luxuriant theme of man's inherent sanctity, echoing through the annals of Church teaching and guiding the moral compass of the faithful.

Insights from Church Fathers

As we delve deeper into the theological wellsprings of human dignity, we uncover the profound musings of the venerable Church Fathers. Their sagacious writings illuminate the inherent worth bestowed upon mankind by the Divine. From the eloquent homilies of John Chrysostom to the profound theological treatises of Augustine, these early Christian luminaries envisaged the human person as a reflection of God's own image. They eloquently expounded upon the intrinsic value of each soul, emphasizing the divine spark within, and thus ardently defending the sanctity of life against all degradations. Their teachings form a golden thread in the grand tapestry of our Church's enduring advocacy for human dignity, portraying it not merely as a philosophical ideal, but as a sacred truth woven into the very fabric of existence.

Augustine's Views on Human Nature shedeth profound illumination upon the concept of human dignity, viewed through the lens of a theological microscope. Indeed, as St. Augustine doth unravel the depths of mankind's essence, he grants us the vantage to espy our true worth as creatures fashioned in God's image. Subtly nuanced, yet crystalline in its profundity, his perspective doth weave an intricate tapestry interlacing sin, grace, and redemption.

In delving into Augustine's magnum opus, "Confessions," one encounters his expounding upon the inherent duality of human existence. Augustine's poignant reflections unfurl the paradox of our nature: a blend of grandeur and frailty, splendor and sin. He doth opine that man is created good, in the likeness of the Almighty, but through Adam's original sin, he hath fallen from grace, thereby tainting his very essence. This fallibility, inherent in each soul, clouds the pristine image of Divine goodness with the murk of iniquity.

Engrossed in the serpentine coils of his profound theologizings, one apprehends that Augustine discerneth human nature through the prism of concupiscence—man's proclivity towards sin. This proclivity, intrinsic to our post-lapsarian state, dost not annihilate human dignity but maketh its preservation paramount. Indeed, it is within this maelstrom of moral struggle that Augustine discerns the potential for divine grace to act as a salve. In this regard, his insights proffer a delicate balance betwixt recognition of human frailty and affirmation of our intrinsic worth.

Augustine perceiveth the human soul as a battleground where virtues and vices waged war, yet he doth also affirm the human capacity for redemption. His ruminations encapsulate his belief in the necessity of grace to transcend sinfulness. Without grace, the human soul remains ensnared in a state of perpetual discord, but with divine aid, it ascends towards the fulfillment of its God-given dignity. This dialectic of sin and grace forms the bedrock of his anthropology, illuminating human worth through both fragility and the potential for transcendence.

Moreover, Augustine's philosophical musings on free will perpetually echo through the corridors of theological discourse. He averreth that free will is a testament to human dignity, for it mirrors the volitional freedom of the Divine Creator. The capacity to choose, even if marred by concupiscence, betokens a latent nobility within mankind. In wielding our will rightly, we reflect the majesty of our Maker. Thus, Augustine doth uphold that free will, even when it leads to sin, doth not negate human dignity but rather underscores our likeness to the Divine.

As Augustine delineates in "City of God," the telos, or ultimate end of human existence, is communion with God. This eschatological vision tempers earthly predicates and lends weight to human dignity. Though man's temporal life be fraught with tribulations and moral dilemmas, his ultimate purpose is otherworldly. Augustine thus asserts that human dignity is not solely predicated upon earthly achievements or moral perfection but upon the eternal destiny in which humanity is called to partake.

Augustine's reflections are not bereft of a sense of community. He envisages the human person not as an isolated monad but as a member of both the "City of God" and the "City of Man." His ecclesiological thought underscores the communal dimension of human dignity. In the fellowship of believers, individuals are edified and sustained by shared faith, love, and grace. The sanctity of human life thus finds expression in communal worship, mutual edification, and collective hope for redemption.

Furthermore, Augustine's insights are inexorably linked to his own grapplings with faith and reason. He doth illustrate through his intellectual journey that faith, far from being antithetical to reason, hath the power to elucidate truths about human nature that reason alone may obfuscate. This union of faith and intellect elevates the human spirit, offering a holistic comprehension of dignity that encompasseth both the material and the transcendent.

Noteworthy is his treatise on the image of God, or Imago Dei, within man. Augustine articulateth that this divine image, while distorted by sin, remaineth an indelible aspect of mankind. It endows us with rationality, morality, and the capacity for relationship with the Divine. Even in our fragmented state, this intrinsic worth and potential for communion with

God imbues human life with an irrefutable dignity. Man, therefore, remains a being of profound worth even amidst imperfection.

To elucidate Augustine's view on human dignity further, one must not overlook his doctrine of original sin. In his exegesis of Holy Writ, Augustine underscores that original sin hath rendered humanity incapable of attaining righteousness by its own merits. This incapacitation underscores our profound need for divine grace. Yet, it is through this recognition of our limitations and God's boundless mercy that human dignity is truly magnified. The redemption offered by Christ bolstereth the worth of every soul, regardless of its fallen state.

In a world that often measures worth by earthly achievements, Augustine's teachings remind us of an inherent dignity rooted not in transitory successes but in our Creator. The divine spark within each person, though hidden beneath the soot of sin, is a testament to an ineffable worth. Augustine's views on human nature challenge us to look beyond the immediate and recognize the eternal significance imbued within every human life.

His emphasis on the transformative power of grace illustrates a dynamic view of human dignity. Augustine sees each person not merely as they are but as they might become through divine aid. Grace, for Augustine, is the great equalizer, offering redemption and dignity to all, irrespective of their past. This vision of transformative potential encourages a view of human nature that is hopeful and redemptive, acknowledging our flaws yet emphasizing our capacity for holiness.

Ultimately, Augustine's ruminations beckon us to a humble acknowledgment of our dependency on God. His anthropology is not a deterministic fatalism but a hopeful trust in divine providence. By embracing both our fragility and our capacity for greatness through grace, we find an authentic understanding of human dignity that nourishes both individual and communal life. Augustine's reflections thus serve as a clarion call to recognize the enduring worth of every human soul and the boundless possibilities for redemption endowed by Divine mercy.

In summation, St. Augustine's theological insights proffer an invaluable compass for navigating the complexities of human nature and dignity. His perspectives, steeped in profound wisdom and spiritual depth, guide us toward a recognition of our intrinsic worth while acknowledging our dependence on divine grace. Through Augustine's timeless teachings, we are reminded that human dignity, far from being a mere philosophical abstraction, is a divine truth inscribed within the very fabric of our being.

Aquinas' Concept of the Sacred Person continues to be a wellspring of theological insight, particularly in the realm of human dignity. As we traverse the hallowed corridors of Aquinas' thought, we find ourselves contemplating the divine mystery of the human person as a sacred entity, a credo enshrined in the ethereal union of the Aquinate's metaphysical principles with his ethical doctrines.

Aquinas posits that the human person, being imago Dei, imbued with the image of God, inherently possesses an unspeakable sanctity. This divine imprint within each soul calls forth an utmost reverence, transcending temporal existence and worldly valuations. Fortified by his synthesis of Aristotelian philosophy and Christian doctrine, Aquinas articulates a vision of humanity as a unique amalgam of body and soul.

Contemplating Aquinas' intellectual edifice, one perceives that human beings, unlike any other creatures, are creatures of reason and free will, qualities that mirror the divine nature. This endowment confers upon them an exalted station in the created order, demanding an ethical response commensurate with their inherent dignity.

The notion of the sacred person in Aquinas' thought is not merely an abstraction but a practical cornerstone of moral action. Through the interplay of intellectual reflection and theological revelation, Aquinas arrives at the profound conclusion that the dignity of the human person is rooted not solely in capability or social status, but in the very act of divine creation itself. Each human life is thus sanctified, a testament to the divine artist's masterpiece.

Within Aquinas' framework, the ensoulment of the human body is a pivotal concept that elevates human dignity. The soul, as the form of the body, invigorates and animates it, directing it toward its ultimate end: the Beatific Vision, the direct encounter with God. Therefore, every human act, every ethical decision, is suffused with the dignity that stems from one's capacity to attain this ultimate union with the Divine.

Moving further, the Summa Theologica unveils Aquinas' holistic perspective on human dignity. He expounds that the rational soul's faculties — intellect and will — are divinely oriented toward truth and goodness. This orientation is not simply extrinsic but intrinsic to the human being, involving deeply interwoven dimensions of moral and intellectual virtues that must be cultivated to realize true personhood.

Hence, the Thomistic view mandates a moral imperative to treat each person as an end in themselves, never as a mere means. This principle echoes through the annals of Catholic teaching, rooting itself deeply in the ethical pulses of personalism and social justice that the Church enshrines.

The sacredness of the human person also finds expression in Aquinas' treatment of law and morality. He delineates the natural law as a participation in the eternal law, inscribing within every person an innate knowledge of good and evil. This internal moral compass upholds human dignity by aligning human conduct with divine wisdom.

To illustrate, Aquinas affirms that all acts detrimental to human life, whether arising from societal injustice or personal sin, starkly contradict this intrinsic knowledge and the sacred worth of the person. Laws and policies that denigrate or diminish human dignity are thus decried as inherently unjust and must be reformed to reflect the divine order of love and justice.

Furthermore, in accurate discernment, Aquinas speaks to the essential community of persons. His concept of the "common good" interlaces the dignity of the individual with the welfare of the community, affirming that personal sanctity and communal justice are inextricably bound. This dimension of Aquinian thought invites us to consider the societal structures that either enhance or undermine the sacredness of the human person.

Aquinas' theology does not end in theoretical musing but calls forth a lived experience of reverence toward human dignity. His reflections challenge the faithful to embody the virtues of justice, charity, and humility, recognizing in every encounter the face of Christ, in whom human dignity finds its fullest revelation and most compelling expression.

Indeed, the profound understanding of the sacredness of the human person in Aquinas' thought beckons modern moral theologians, Roman Catholics, and sociologists alike to delve deeper into the moral teachings of the Church, advocating steadfastly for the inviolable dignity of every human life. It is a clarion call to animate our actions with the spirit of love and justice, honoring the divine mystery inscribed within each person.

Modern Theological Developments

In the parlance of contemporary theology, much hath arisen to reaffirm and elucidate the intrinsic worth of the human person, as anchored in the venerable teachings of the Church. The Second Vatican Council, a watershed in ecclesiastical history, promulgated profound insights on the nature of human dignity, accentuating the image of God reflected in each soul. No longer ensnared solely in august philosophical treatises or ancient dogmas, this modern elucidation extends its reach to address the exigencies of an ever-evolving society, blending timeless truths with the cadence of current discourse. Thus, it is with a heart wrought in conviction that the Church endeavors to illuminate the sanctity of human life amidst the contemporary whirlwind, reaffirming that every individual, adorned with the imago Dei, is worthy of utmost reverence and sanctity.

Vatican II and the Human Person rests upon the critical soul of modern theological developments. This august assembly sought to rediscover the luminance of human dignity and underscore its indispensability to theological discourse. The Second Vatican Council, convened betwixt 1962 and 1965, was a clarion call to examine human existence anew. It championed the inalienable dignity and inviolable worth intrinsic to every human person.

One must cast an eye upon the Council's foundational documents to unveil its perspective on human dignity. "Gaudium et Spes," the Pastoral Constitution on the Church in the Modern World, emerged as a touchstone for understanding the Church's rearticulated views. Employed was language imbued with both compassion and solemn reflection, exhorting humanity to acknowledge its divine origin and ultimate destiny. Herein, the Church posited that the human person, crafted in the imago Dei, bore an inherent dignity that transcended all earthly valuations.

Vatican II's declaration that individuals possess dignity simply by virtue of their humanity marked an epochal shift; no longer would the Church's teachings be shrouded merely in the grandeur of the saints or enshrined in sacramental solemnities. The Council addressed itself to the modern individual—fraught with existential anxieties yet yearning for existential purpose. Such declarations imprinted upon the ecclesiastical consciousness an urgent appeal for universal respect and fundamental rights.

Moreover, "Dignitatis Humanae," the Declaration on Religious Freedom, was instrumental in cementing the Council's stance on human dignity. It contended that freedom of conscience is imperative to uphold the sanctity of the human person. The Council thus enjoined states and societies to uphold and protect this sacred right. No longer could humanity's spiritual inclinations be restrained by the fetters of coercive regimes.

The Council Fathers also endeavored to reconcile the human proclivity toward error with the notion of unconditional dignity. By recognizing humanity's intrinsic fallibility, Vatican II espoused a theology that was both realistic and hopeful. It gestured toward an embrace of mercy, underscoring that human dignity remains unscathed by imperfection or sin. This paradigm shift invigorated pastoral pursuits, exhorting clergy and laity alike to extend unconditional love and respect unto one another.

The concept of 'communitarian dignity' was another pivotal innovation. The Council highlighted that relationality and community are indispensable to understanding individual dignity. The human person is not an isolated monad but a being-in-relationship, forged within the crucible of communal ties. Hence, the promotion of the common good became an ethical imperative, arising from the acknowledgment that one's dignity is integrally connected to the dignity of all.

Furthermore, Vatican II urged an engagement with contemporary scientific and philosophical advancements, insisting that these domains of human understanding could coalesce harmoniously with theological truths. Herein lies a celebration of human rationality and creativity as aspects of one's divine image, stipulating that scientific inquiry should serve the holistic dignity of the person. The Church, therefore, emerged not as an adversary to reason but as its auxiliary, tasked with guiding human intellect toward truths that nourish human dignity.

On matters of social justice, Vatican II was unambiguous. The Council invoked the Beatitudes as a clarion call to honor the dignity of the poor, the marginalized, and the oppressed. It declared that any affront to human dignity in any quarter was an affront to the divine Creator. Such proclamations galvanized movements for justice, peace, and human rights, infusing them with theological legitimacy.

Thus, the Council's elucidation on human dignity had both ecclesial and societal ramifications. It energized Catholic social teaching and emboldened the Church to partake in dialogues on human rights, justice, and peace. The ramifications of Vatican II's teachings seeped into the moral imaginations of both the lay faithful and the wider world, situating the Church as a bulwark for human dignity in an age of burgeoning secularism and moral indecision.

In synthesizing the Council Fathers' contributions, one beholds a profound testament to humanity's unrivaled worth. The Second Vatican Council heralded a renaissance in theological anthropology, reawakening the Church and world to the profundity of the human person. It summoned Christians to ethical integrity and unyielding advocacy for human dignity, echoing through the annals of ecclesiastical history.

Yet, even as one venerates the past, the spirit of Vatican II beckons the modern Church to persist in its mission. It beckons us to ever purify our vision and labor tirelessly for a world in which every human person, irrespective of creed, race, or circumstance, is honored as a reflection of the sacred. By rooting our endeavors in this profound understanding of human dignity, we continue to traverse the ecclesial pilgrimage with hearts awash in divine love and minds fervent for justice.

The theological vision of Vatican II, thus, remains a lodestar—a guiding light in the moral and spiritual odyssey of contemporary Catholicism. Holding fast to these teachings, the Church journeys forward, with unwavering resolve to hallow every life as a vessel of divine grace and truth.

Chapter 3: Philosophical Underpinnings of Dignity

As we traverse from the theological precepts ingrained by the Church Fathers, we embark now upon the philosophical terrain that profoundly etched the essence of human dignity into the annals of human thought. The ancients—Aristotle amongst them—conferred upon us the principle that man's rational soul renders him unique, lifting him above the mere animals. Such an elevation implies an intrinsic worth, a mirror reflecting divine semblance. Likewise, the Stoics, with their call to harmony with natural law and virtue, paved the path for an understanding that our inherent dignity stems from our capacity for reason and moral judgment. In modern epochs, Personalism elucidates this philosophy further; in its assertion, every individual, as an unrepeatable entity, holds intrinsic value that no external circumstances can diminish. Thus, the philosophical inquiry, entwined with rich, variegated threads of the classic and the contemporary, fortifies the edifice of human dignity, aligning it seamlessly with the moral teachings embraced by the Church.

Classical Philosophical Influences

The mantle of dignity finds its earliest threads in the classical tapestry of philosophical wisdom, woven by the venerable hands of thinkers such as Socrates, Plato, Aristotle, and the Stoics. These ancient sages, through the prism of reason and virtue, beheld the inherent worth of the human soul, functioning as geistlich forebears to the Church's later explications of human dignity. Aristotle, with his doctrines of telos and eudaimonia, accentuated the flourishing intrinsic to human nature, positing dignity as not merely an abstract ideal but a tangible outcome of virtuous living. The Stoics, in parallel harmony, espoused the universality of reason, affirming that each person, by sheer presence of rational intellect, partakes in a cosmic dignity. Thus, these classical minds served as philosophical cornerstones, laying the groundwork upon which the edifice of Catholic moral teaching would majestically rise, etching the concept of dignity into the very essence of human existence, a notion sanctified and profound.

Aristotle's Contribution spans the annals of classical wisdom, a beacon in the corridors of the mind, shedding light upon the profound nature of human dignity. Born in Stagira, this illustrious thinker shaped the contours of philosophical inquiry, proffering notions that resonate deeply within the moral teachings embraced by the Church. His reflections on the inherent worth of the human person contribute significantly to our understanding in the "Philosophical Underpinnings of Dignity."

Perchance the heart of Aristotle's philosophic endeavors lies in his contemplation of the "rational soul." He posited that man's unique capacity for reason distinguished him not merely as an animal, but as an entity imbued with intrinsic worth. The rational faculty, Aristotle asserted, permits the pursuit of truth, virtue, and eudaimonia—human flourishing. Thus, in recognizing man's potential for rationality, one cannot but infer his dignity.

In "Nicomachean Ethics," Aristotle delineates the concept of virtue, intricately linking it to the soul's rational activity. To live virtuously, according to Aristotle, is to live in accordance with reason, which bestows upon every man an undeniable dignity. Virtue, he avowed, exists as the mean between excess and deficiency—a golden mean that requires the engagement of human intellect and will. Herein lies a cornerstone of moral theology: the pursuit of virtue is fundamental to acknowledging and upholding human dignity.

Moreover, Aristotle's disquisition on politics contributes richly to our discourse on dignity. He perceived the city-state as a natural community aimed at achieving the good life—a shared existence oriented towards virtuous living. The inherent dignity of individuals finds its expression in the political realm, where the collective pursuit of the common good elevates personal worth. For Aristotle, the polity exists not for mere survival, but for the realization of the highest potentials of human nature.

In examining Aristotle's "Politics," one observes his endorsement of the necessity of justice—a precept central to the Church's moral teachings. Justice, which Aristotle deemeth as both a personal virtue and a social necessity, affirms the dignity of every person by fostering an environment where each can achieve virtue. His assertion that "the law is reason unaffected by desire" underscores the imperative of unbiased governance, a principle echoed in the Church's advocacy for social justice.

Importantly, Aristotle's notion of friendship ("philia") further elucidates the concept of human dignity. He contended that true friendship is founded upon mutual recognition of the good within each person. This recognition begets respect, an acknowledgment indispensable to the concept of dignity. Friends, in valuing one another's virtues and rational capacities, serve as reflections of each other's intrinsic worth. Such relationships, grounded in Aristotle's ethical framework, enhance the understanding of community and interpersonal respect within Catholic thought.

Aristotle's meditations on the soul, and its faculties, compel a reverent examination. The tripartite structure of the soul—vegetative, appetitive, and rational—finds harmony in the pursuit of the good. The dominance of the rational over the irrational parts serves as a testament to human dignity. Such a view echoes throughout the Church's teachings, underscoring the sanctity of life as not merely biological existence but as a deliberate, rational, and virtuous engagement with God's creation.

Within the thicket of Aristotelian ethics stands the imposing figure of the "magnanimous man." This archetype, possessed of virtue, wisdom, and nobility, provides an ideal for human comportment. Magnanimity, characterized by an acknowledgment of one's worth and the duty to act in accordance with that worth, mirrors the Catholic understanding of man's inherent dignity and his call to live as a testament to God's glory. Aristotle's magnanimous man serves as a template, guiding Catholics to appreciate their worth and strive for greatness.

The essence of Aristotle's philosophy radiates through his conception of teleology—the belief that all things have an end goal or purpose. For Aristotle, humanity's telos lies in achieving eudaimonia through virtuous living. This teleological perspective dovetails exquisitely with the Church's teachings on human dignity, which also emphasize purposeful living in alignment with divine will. The conviction that every human life possesses a divinely ordained purpose compels a recognition of its inherent worth.

Furthermore, Aristotle's impact resonates in the realm of metaphysics, where his reflections on substance and essence imbue our comprehension of dignity with profundity. Man, as an individual substance of a rational nature, exists not as a mere composite of matter and form, but as a unique instantiation of a divinely willed essence. This conception underscores the Church's position that human dignity transcends physical attributes and socioeconomic conditions, rooting it instead in the very nature of one's being.

Finally, the synthesis of Aristotelian thought with Christian theology demands mention. The labors of St. Thomas Aquinas, infused with Aristotelian philosophy, render a harmonious union between reason and faith. By integrating Aristotle's insights on human nature, Aquinas fortified the Church's understanding of dignity. He reiterated that reason and revelation together illuminate the pathway to recognizing the divine image in every person, a cornerstone of Catholic doctrine.

Thus do we observe Aristotle's indelible imprint upon the philosophical foundation of human dignity, seamlessly woven into the fabric of Catholic moral teaching. His extensive exploration of reason, virtue, and the purpose of human life stands as a testament to the inviolable worth of the human person. The Church, in her wisdom, draws from this wellspring of knowledge, affirming that every individual, by virtue of their rational soul and purposeful existence, is endowed with a dignity that calls for protection, respect, and reverence.

Stoic Views on Human Nature In the labyrinthine corridors of philosophy, the echoes of the Stoics resound with a dignified cadence. Their discourse, exquisitely rational yet phosphorescent with profound sympathy, best exposes the Stoic reverence for human nature while embedding itself firmly in the bedrock of our intrinsic dignity. Stoicism graces us with the celestial insight that human beings, regardless of their outward condition, possess an enduring and inviolable worth. Their discourse on nature, virtue, and reason frames this venerable heritage of human dignity, standing as sentinels at the gates of our moral and existential inquiries.

Esteemed thinkers like Seneca, Epictetus, and Marcus Aurelius elaborated on the grandeur of our character, presenting it as unassailable under the vicissitudes of fortune. Virtue, as proclaimed by the Stoics, is the sole good, and vice the sole evil, thereby placing great emphasis on moral integrity above all else. They saw each human being as a microcosm of the grander cosmos, a miniature representation of rational order and divine intelligence. In this light, our worth is not contingent on external markers of success or failure but instead nestled within our capacity for reason, moral autonomy, and alignment with nature's order.

The Stoics posited that every soul, irrespective of its external fortunes, has a spark of divine rationality. This rationality connects us to a larger, universal order, an assertion that human dignity is anchored in our participation in a cosmos teeming with reason and purpose. Such a perspective not only calls upon individuals to cultivate their inner virtues but also to recognize the innate worth in others, fostering a sense of moral kinship and universal fellowship.

In the Stoic worldview, the sage—one who attains moral and intellectual perfection—exemplifies the highest form of human dignity through the harmonious cultivation of reason. Unlike other philosophical schools that might tether worth to social status, material wealth, or physical beauty, Stoicism entrenches dignity in the immutable realm of virtue. It asserts that true freedom comes not from external circumstances but from inner moral clarity and strength.

Moreover, the Stoics herald an inexorable truth that life itself is neither good nor evil. Rather, it is how one lives it—guided by virtue and in accordance with nature—that renders existence meaningful. This philosophical stance, stern yet liberating, challenges us to transcend our temporal trials and tribulations, no matter how dire. In so doing, we discover that dignity is not the remnant of our survival but its very essence.

One cannot broach the Stoic understanding of human nature without encountering their famed acceptance of fate—Amor Fati. This heartfelt embracement of one's lot in life teaches us that human dignity springs not from rebellion against our circumstances but from a profound acceptance and transcendence of them. By aligning with the rational order of the universe, we reflect the divine intelligence that suffuses all existence, granting us an indelible worth and purpose.

This alignment is not passive acquiescence but an active engagement in life. The Stoics implore us to 'act well the given part,' to exercise our rational faculties, to practice justice, courage, temperance, and wisdom, regardless of the circumstances we find ourselves in. This adheres closely to the Christian ethos that asserts the sanctity and dignity of human life in every condition, from the heights of joy to the depths of suffering.

The Stoic emphasis on community offers a vital complement to their views on individual human dignity. By envisioning humanity as a singular, interconnected entity, they encourage us to view every person, regardless of social distinctions, as a fellow participant in the divine logos. This cosmopolitan bond stands as a precursor to the Catholic idea of the Mystical Body of Christ, wherein each member is invaluable to the whole, rich with purpose and dignity.

In their teachings, justice extends beyond personal virtue to social obligation. This aspect positions the Stoics as precursors to modern discussions on human rights and social justice. They remind us that our individual moral integrity has societal implications, urging a view of dignity that is both personal and communal. Through justice, we acknowledge not only our own worth but also the inherent dignity of every other person, advocate for their rights, and work towards the common good.

It is fitting then, to contemplate how Stoic thought interfaces with the moral teachings of the Church. The Stoics' call to live in harmony with nature, to cultivate inner virtue, and to recognize the inherent worth in all humans finds an echo in the fundamental Christian principles of love, compassion, and inherent human dignity. In this shared philosophical and theological landscape, we find fertile ground for a robust apology of human dignity, a testament to our shared moral heritage and destiny.

In conclusion, Stoic views on human nature unfold a panorama where each person's dignity is underscored by their participation in a rational, ordered cosmos. This perspective not only aligns harmoniously with but also enriches the Church's teachings on human dignity. It invites us to enter deeper dimensions of moral reflection, urging us to live virtuously and recognize the divine spark within every human soul. Through such understanding, we can better advocate for human dignity in a world that increasingly seeks to define worth by transient measures.

Contemporary Philosophical Approaches

In the realm of contemporary philosophy, the discourse on human dignity has found a fertile ground for exploration and robust expansion. By championing the intrinsic worth of the individual, modern philosophical currents such as personalism delve deeply into the nature of the person as an unrepeatable subject, endowed with a unique value transcending mere utility. This approach aligns profoundly with the Catholic understanding of man as imago Dei, a reflection of the divine image imbued with an inalienable dignity. These philosophical perspectives do not merely uphold dignity as an abstract concept; rather, they weave it into the very fabric of human existence, asserting that dignity constitutes the bedrock of ethical interactions and moral imperatives. Thus, in juxtaposing classical and modern thoughts, one finds a resplendent tapestry that underscores the perennial importance of dignity, reverberating through the ages and setting the stage for a theological and moral synthesis that is both compelling and cohesive.

Personalism and Its Relevance emerges as a luminous cornerstone amid the labyrinthine corridors of contemporary philosophical approaches. Rooted in the very soil that bore the fruits of classical thought, Personalism, nonetheless, blossoms uniquely, offering a nuanced voice on the dignity of the human person. As a philosophical lens attuned to the intrinsic worth of human existence, it intersects compellingly with the Roman Catholic understanding of moral theology, resonating deeply within the tapestry of the Church's teachings.

At its heart, Personalism emphasizes the irreplaceable value of the individual. It exhorts us to acknowledge the human person not merely as an abstract entity within a collective but as a singular, dignified being imbued with reason, will, and moral responsibility. This is a clarion call to reflect on the sanctity of each life, where no person is deemed expendable or secondary. The echoes of this thought find their origins in the whispers of antiquity, yet in their modern articulation, they speak robustly to our contemporary sensibilities.

Personalism draws a vivid line against the mechanistic and utilitarian views that pervade much of modern secular philosophy. Where utilitarianism might calculate worth based on utility, Personalism insists on the inherent dignity of the human soul. The person, in the Personalist framework, possesses a moral and spiritual depth that transcends mere functional attributes. It is in this light that one perceives the profound affinity between Personalism and the Church's teachings on human dignity; both uphold the innate value bestowed by the Creator upon every individual.

The relevance of Personalism in today's ethical landscape cannot be overstated. Contemporary issues, from bioethics to social justice, necessitate a framework that situates human dignity at the forefront of moral deliberations. Personalism provides such a framework, offering a potent antidote to the pervasive cultures of commodification and dehumanization. By safeguarding the dignity of the marginalized and the vulnerable, it echoes the Church's call to uphold the sanctity of life in all its stages—from conception to natural death.

Furthermore, Personalism's emphasis on relationality aligns harmoniously with the Catholic notion of community and communion. It posits that individuals realize their fullness not in isolation, but in relationship with others, echoing the Trinitarian nature of God Himself. This provides a fertile ground for engaging with social doctrines such as solidarity and subsidiarity, terms deeply embedded within the fabric of Catholic social teaching.

One must also consider how Personalism interacts with the advancements in science and technology that define our age. Genetic engineering, artificial intelligence, and other frontier sciences pose significant ethical dilemmas concerning human dignity. Personalism, with its unwavering focus on the person, offers guiding principles that can help navigate these turbulent waters. It urges caution and reverence, challenging us to consider the moral implications of reducing humans to mere subjects of technological manipulation or economic calculus.

Moreover, Personalism finds resounding affirmation in the Church's magisterial documents. The Second Vatican Council, particularly in Gaudium et Spes, underlined the profound dignity and vocation of the human person. This magisterial endorsement serves as a bridge, linking theological and philosophical discourses, and thereby enriching the Church's apologetic mission. Through such alignment, Personalism not only reinforces but also elucidates the Church's moral teachings, rendering them more intelligible and compelling to the contemporary mind.

The synthesis of Personalism with ecclesial teachings also sheds light on ethical issues surrounding life. Issues such as abortion and euthanasia are not merely debates on legality but moral outcries where the dignity of the human person is in jeopardy. Personalism fortifies the Church's stance by arguing that every life holds a unique, unrepeatable significance that goes beyond societal and utilitarian considerations. This perspective insists on the cherishment of life at its most vulnerable stages, mirroring the Church's profound commitment to the protection of the unborn and the elderly.

In grappling with the moral crises of our time, Personalism does not shy away from confronting systemic injustices. It recognizes that societal structures often undermine human dignity, thereby calling for transformation that reflects the essential worth of every person. This resonates with the Church's preferential option for the poor and its advocacy for social justice. Personalism and Catholic social teaching together advocate for environments where each person's dignity can flourish, free from oppression and despair.

Therefore, in addressing the burdens of our present age, Personalism beckons to both the individual and the collective conscience. It serves as a philosophical bulwark, protecting against the erosion of human dignity by contemporary cultural currents. As such, it offers a robust foundation for moral theologians, sociologists, and the faithful to reflect upon and defend the sacred value of human life.

In conclusion, Personalism, with its rich philosophical lineage and profound moral implications, stands as a beacon in the quest for understanding and upholding human dignity. Its relevance resonates through the corridors of time, invoking a call to honor the sanctity and worth of each person, aligning seamlessly with the timeless moral teachings of the Church. Through this potent confluence, we find a compelling vision that not only fortifies the Church's mission but also offers a luminous path forward for humanity's moral journey.

Chapter 4: Moral Teachings of the Church

The sacred enterprise of delineating the moral teachings of the Church finds its genesis in the divine command, summoning forth an august responsibility upon each soul to navigate the turbulent seas of ethical dilemmas with celestial compass. Most profound among these doctrines are the Ten Commandments, etching in eternal stone the divine will, guiding human comportment towards righteousness. Augmenting these ancient decrees, the Catechism stands as an edifice of moral instruction, illuminating the path for the faithful through the chiaroscuro of contemporary life. Bioethical quandaries, bespeaking the essence of human dignity at its very zenith, embolden the Church's unwavering stance in safeguarding life from the first breath to the last sigh. Moreover, the clarion call toward social justice admonishes believers to not only seek but advocate a moral society that upholds the sacredness of every individual, echoing the storied virtue of compassion. These teachings, thus, form a tapestry woven with threads of divine instruction and human aspiration, ever pointing towards the celestial harmony ordained by our Creator.

Central Doctrines on Morality

In the vast tapestry of moral thought, the Church's central doctrines unravel as threads of divine wisdom, weaving together the ethical fabric that guides the faithful. Anchored by the Ten Commandments and expounded through the Catechism, these doctrines illuminate the path to virtuous living, transcending temporal constraints and anchoring the soul in eternal truths. The Church, with her magisterial authority, delineates clear moral imperatives, urging adherence to principles that honor the intrinsic worth of every human person. At the heart of these teachings lies the unequivocal assertion of human dignity, a testament to humanity's divine imprint and a clarion call to uphold justice, mercy, and love in all interactions. These tenets, robust in their theological underpinnings and philosophical coherence, serve as a bulwark against moral relativism, beckoning the believer to a higher standard of holiness and righteousness. In embracing these truths, one finds not merely a code of conduct but an invitation to participate in the divine life, echoing the celestial harmony ordained by the Creator.

The Ten Commandments and Human Behavior serve as the ultimate guideposts for charting the complex waters of human morality, embodying the essence of divine wisdom encapsulated in God's law. To the faithful, these edicts are not merely historical artifacts but vibrant, pulsating directives that govern the contours of human interaction. Their relevance transcends temporal confines, piercing the fabric of modern existence with poignant resonance.

In examining the ethical dimension of the Decalogue, one must attest to its unparalleled influence on the gradations of human conduct. Each commandment unfolds as a profound moral proposition, a syllogism of divine perfection, endeavoring to sculpt us into beings of elevated virtue. The injunctions against idolatry, false witness, and covetousness, amongst others, delineate a code of conduct that enhances the dignity inherent in every individual.

Thou shalt have no other gods before Me. This paramount command underscores the principle of monotheism, crystallizing the need for an exclusive loyalty to the one true God. It is not merely a prohibition but an invitation to recognize a higher order of morality, an oracle that beckons mortals to transcend the mundane and embrace the sacred.

The interdiction against idolatry, likewise, serves as a metaphysical anchor, disavowing the material as ultimate. Idolatry, whether manifest in graven images or material obsessions, diverts humans from their inherent purpose and dignity. Herein lies a sublime call to a life of simplicity and spiritual depth, away from the cacophonous clamor of transient pleasures and toward the eternal hymn of divine love.

In a similar vein, the commandment to honor thy father and mother encapsulates the essence of familial respect, a cornerstone of social cohesion. This edict transcends mere dutiful compliance, enshrining a philosophy that nurtures generational continuity and relational integrity. It fosters an environment wherein individuals, young and old, recognize their place in the intricate tapestry of human existence, thereby preserving the sanctity of the family unit.

Thou shalt not kill. The significance of this commandment cannot be overstated, for it preserves the inviolable sanctity of life. In a world that grapples with manifold forms of violence and ethical quandaries surrounding life and death, this divine injunction acts as a bulwark. It asserts the intrinsic value of each human life, urging a collective moral awakening against the culture of death that pervades contemporary society. Truly, this proclamation stands as a beacon of hope for a more compassionate world.

Moreover, commandments prohibiting theft and false witness lay the foundations for societal justice and ethical interactions. These edicts engender trust and authenticity, vital components for a functioning, harmonious community. To live by these precepts is to embody the highest form of moral accountability, ensuring that one's actions contribute to the common good rather than undermining it.

The final commandments, which address covetousness of one's neighbor's goods or spouse, delve deep into the human soul, admonishing us against the corrosive nature of envy and material desire. Covetousness enslaves the heart, making one a prisoner of insatiable wanting. This commandment invites believers to seek contentment and purity of intention, thus fortifying the inner sanctum of the human spirit against the depredations of worldly greed.

Essentially, the Decalogue doesn't function merely as a set of prohibitions but as a framework for authentic freedom. In adhering to these divine statutes, individuals are liberated from the bondage of moral confusion, aligning themselves with a higher, more fulfilling order of existence. This forms the core of the Church's moral teachings, where the Ten Commandments resonate as eternal principles that shape the very essence of human dignity.

In an age beset by ethical relativism, the Ten Commandments serve as a clarion call to steadfast moral integrity. They stand in stark contrast to the ephemeral nature of human-made laws, which are often swayed by the fickle tides of cultural and societal change. Indeed, the Decalogue's timeless wisdom remains an unwavering guide, providing a moral compass that directs human behavior toward the divine telos.

Through the Ten Commandments, the Church imparts a moral vision that sees beyond the temporal realm, anchoring human behavior in eternal truth. No less than this is required, for the journey toward sainthood demands a roadmap, illuminated by the same divine commands given to Moses upon Sinai's hallowed summit. It is within this framework that human dignity finds its fullest expression.

Furthermore, the Decalogue dovetails seamlessly with the broader expanse of ethical teachings found in the Catechism, which further elucidates these principles within the context of contemporary moral dilemmas. The Catechism acts as a magnifier, casting the ancient commandments into modern relief, thus making them accessible to present-day moral theology.

Ultimately, adherence to the Ten Commandments enriches the human soul, fostering a community where dignity and virtue coexist harmoniously. Each commandment, therefore, is not a mere rule to be followed but a divine lath, crafting the moral contours of human behavior. To observe these commandments is to embark upon a pilgrimage toward ultimate human fulfillment, guided by the divine hand that scribed them in the annals of eternity.

The Catechism and Moral Guidance within the labyrinth of ecclesiastical teachings stands as a beacon, illuminating the path of righteousness for the faithful. The Catechism of the Catholic Church, a robust compendium of doctrine, serves as the primary repository of the Church's moral teachings. Rooted in Sacred Scripture, Apostolic Tradition, and the magisterial authority of the Church, it offers a cohesive and coherent framework for understanding divine laws as they pertain to human conduct.

Embedded within its pages, the Catechism intertwines the wisdom of millennia, weaving together the ethical imperatives that shape the moral landscape of Catholic life. It elucidates the commandments, beatitudes, and ecclesial precepts, distilling them into a harmonious symphony of moral directives. The Catechism addresses every facet of human action, binding faith to reason and divine mandate to practical obligation, forming the cornerstone upon which the faithful are called to build their lives.

In asserting the inviolable dignity of the human person, the Catechism becomes a conduit of divine justice, an oracle of the sacred. It speaks not with the transient voice of human philosophy but with the eternal resonance of divine command. Through it, the Church transmits the imperishable truths that govern the actions of mankind, urging a life of virtue and holiness, knit together with threads of charity, justice, and temperance.

One cannot overlook the centrality of the Ten Commandments within the Catechism. These divine edicts, etched into the very fabric of creation, form the bedrock of moral life. They are neither arbitrary decrees nor mere historical artifacts; they resonate deeply with the natural law inscribed upon the human heart. From the reverence due to God to the sanctity of life and the inviolability of truth, the Commandments delineate the moral boundaries within which human freedom may flourish.

Delving deeper, the Catechism elucidates each commandment with meticulous attention, drawing forth principles that govern both interior disposition and outward action. For example, the commandment "Thou shalt not kill" extends beyond the physical act of murder, encompassing the broader spectrum of respect for life. It invites a profound reflection on issues such as abortion, euthanasia, and capital punishment, guiding the faithful towards a posture of respect and protection for all human life.

The Catechism's treatment of moral guidance does not halt at the commandments alone; it ventures forth into the realm of the beatitudes, unveiling the sublime paradoxes of Christian morality. "Blessed are the poor in spirit, for theirs is the kingdom of heaven." Here, the Catechism reveals the transformative power of humility and detachment, prompting the faithful to seek treasures not of this world but of the divine kingdom. The beatitudes, therefore, become a roadmap to sanctity, encouraging an ethos of meekness, mercy, and purity of heart that stands in stark contrast to secular values.

Moreover, the Catechism serves as a critical tool for moral catechesis, instructing the conscience and fortifying the moral fiber of both the laity and clergy. It provides a structured and thorough exposition of virtues and vices, echoing the ancient teachings of the Church Fathers. Virtues like prudence, justice, fortitude, and temperance are explored in conjunction, compelling the faithful toward a life of moral excellence, while the intricacies of sin and its consequences are meticulously unwrapped, highlighting the gravity of moral transgressions and the imperative for repentance.

However, the guidance proffered by the Catechism is not limited to the austerity of legalistic adherence. It embraces the pastoral dimension, recognizing the complexity of human circumstances and the nuances of individual conscience. The concept of invincible ignorance finds a place within its text, acknowledging the finite understanding of man and the divine mercy that envelops those who seek truth earnestly. This pastoral care is a testament to the Church's maternal heart, which instructs not through coercion but through love and invitation.

In the context of contemporary moral dilemmas, the Catechism also provides clarity and direction. It addresses bioethical issues that arise from advancements in science and medicine, offering moral principles that safeguard human dignity amidst technological progress. Stem cell research, genetic engineering, and end-of-life issues are examined under the light of the Church's moral teachings, reinforcing a framework that upholds the sacredness of life and the ethical use of human innovation.

A particular emphasis is placed on social justice, reflecting the Church's longstanding commitment to the marginalized and oppressed. The Catechism articulates principles such as the preferential option for the poor and the importance of solidarity and subsidiarity. These teachings compel the faithful to transcend personal interests, advocating for policies and practices that promote the common good and protect human rights. It calls for active participation in societal transformation, echoing Christ's command to love one's neighbor as oneself.

Thus, the Catechism is not an archaic document relegated to the annals of history; it is a vibrant and living testament to the moral wisdom of the Church. It captures the timeless truths of the Gospel while addressing the exigencies of modern life, guiding the faithful in their journey through the moral complexities of this world. It serves both as a mirror that reflects the divine image within man and as a window that opens to the expansive vistas of God's kingdom.

As we navigate the moral terrain delineated by the Catechism, we encounter a dual invitation: to discover the depths of our own dignity and to respect the dignity of others. The moral guidance it offers is not a burden but a path to authentic freedom, one where the human person flourishes in the fullness of truth and love. It beckons us to a higher standard, one ingrained with divine purpose and crowned with eternal reward.

In conclusion, the Catechism of the Catholic Church stands as an indomitable pillar of moral teaching, guiding the faithful through the intricate and oftentimes tumultuous journey of human life. Its teachings, deeply rooted in divine revelation and Church tradition, offer a luminous path to holiness. Through its moral guidance, it affirms the sublime dignity of the human person, calling each to a life of virtue, integrity, and profound respect for the moral order established by God Himself.

Ethical Implications of Church Teachings

Verily, the ethical implications of the Church's moral teachings cast a profound illumination upon the sanctity of human existence. Each doctrine, like a shimmering beacon, guides the faithful through the labyrinthine paths of moral dilemmas, exalting the dignity of all souls. This divine compendium of principles elicits not mere adherence but a transformation of the heart and conscience, urging mankind toward the higher virtues of justice, charity, and respect for life. Inquiries of bioethics spark fervid debates, yet the Church remains resolute, championing the inviolable dignity of the human person against the encroachments of utilitarianism. As the tenets of social justice unfold, they demand a committed embrace of the oppressed and vulnerable, igniting within each person a fervent pursuit of the common good. Thus, the moral teachings transcend mere edict, becoming the very essence of ethical living, molding every action into a testament of unwavering devotion to human dignity.

Bioethics and Human Dignity emerges as a crucial subset of the Church's moral teachings, aligning itself with an unwavering affirmation of the sanctity of human existence. To delve into the depths of bioethics within the realm of ecclesiastical doctrine is to engage in a discourse that transcends mere biological considerations; it embraces the very essence of human identity and the divine nature afforded to every soul. This intersection of ethics and humanity demands a thoughtful exploration through the lens of faith.

The Church's moral teachings are a bulwark against the dehumanizing tendencies of modernity. Bioethics, as understood in this sacred context, is not merely a set of medical dos and don'ts but a holistic approach to human life that reveres the image of God inherent in every person. In the intricate web of moral implications, bioethics radiates the brilliance of divine love manifested in our moral obligations towards the most vulnerable among us.

Human dignity, a concept etched in divine sanction, serves as the cornerstone of bioethical discourse. The Church insists that from conception to natural death, human life holds an unparalleled worth. Thus, the ethical implications of this teaching refute any practices that undermine this inherent dignity. Abortion, euthanasia, and other forms of life manipulation not only pose moral quandaries but starkly conflict with the sacredness attached to human existence. Such perspectives urge a return to valuing life as a divine gift rather than a disposable commodity.

The Church Fathers, especially the likes of Augustine and Aquinas, set poignant precedents in this discussion. Augustine's reflections on humanity's fallen yet redeemable nature and Aquinas' profound assertions on the sacred character of the human person illuminate the theological basis for our modern bioethical understanding. These doctrines articulate an enduring narrative: human dignity is not contingent on utility or social status but is inherently bestowed by divine grace.

Within the sprawling landscape of ethical considerations, contemporary challenges such as genetic engineering, cloning, and end-of-life decisions demand urgent ethical evaluation. The Church's moral teachings act as a compass, directing believers through these complex dilemmas, ensuring that scientific advancement does not trample upon the sanctity of creation. The unwavering stance is clear; human beings must never be treated as mere instruments for technological experimentation but as bearers of the Divine image.

Moreover, the ethical principles propounded by the Church are not confined to overt issues like euthanasia or abortion. They extend their reach to the subtler realms of healthcare delivery, patient care ethics, and the equitable distribution of medical resources. Imperative within this discourse is the call for healthcare practitioners to treat patients with unwavering reverence for their dignity—upholding trust, empathy, and compassion as foundational virtues.

In bioethics, the concept of human dignity often collides with utilitarian perspectives, which may argue for the "greater good" at the expense of the individual. The Church repudiates such arguments by emphasizing that the notion of dignity does not admit of degrees; it is absolute and indivisible. A person's worth is not a balance sheet of contributions, but a given truth derived from God's love.

Furthermore, ethical implications stretch beyond mere policy to personal vocation. Healthcare providers, researchers, and caregivers are called to bear witness to Christ through their vocational conduct. The moral imperatives rooted in Church teaching encourage them to see their work as a form of ministry, a testament to the sanctity of life and the dignity of the human person. Every act of care, every gesture of support becomes imbued with divine significance.

The moral teachings of the Church, especially as they concern bioethics, are designed to uphold a civilization of love. This love manifests in the respect for the elderly, the sick, the unborn, and those on the margins of society. The Church's advocacy for the marginalized reflects a broader ethical imperative: true dignity involves the inclusion of every human person, regardless of their stage in life or their social utility.

Historical precedents and teachings must amalgamate with modern ethical challenges. The Second Vatican Council's teachings underscore a responsible application of emerging technologies, always with an eye toward genuine human flourishing. In doing so, the Church aims to advocate for a balance—a discerning evaluation of technological benefits against the potential risks to human dignity and moral priorities.

In sum, the ethical implications of Church teachings, particularly in the realm of bioethics, affirm a reverence for life that is both philosophical and deeply practical. Every scientific inquiry, every medical advancement, and each bioethical decision must be scrutinized through the prism of human dignity. This unyielding commitment underscores a broader theological and moral vision, one that places the human person, a reflection of the Divine, at the heart of ethical considerations.

The Church's bioethical teachings stand as a testament to the sanctity of life. They challenge us to reexamine our values, our practices, and our very understanding of what it means to be human. In a world rife with moral ambiguities, these teachings offer clarity, grounding us in the eternal truths that transcend temporal concerns. As we navigate the ethical landscape shaped by rapid scientific advancements, the unwavering light of Church doctrine guides us back to the immutable dignity bestowed by the Creator upon every human soul.

Social Justice and Moral Responsibility shine forth as illustrious beacons within the doctrinal tapestry of the Church's moral teachings, occupying a salient position in both ecclesiastical traditions and the ethical sphere. They are not mere abstract notions; rather, they are the lifeblood of Christ's compassionate message, filled with divine imperative. While delving into this subject, one is reminded of the profound words of the Lord, who beckons His followers to 'depart from evil and do good; seek peace and pursue it.' These divine exhortations transcend mere ritual adherence, calling forth an authentic embodiment of God's love through acts of charity and justice.

In the chiaroscuro of history, the Church has ardently illuminated the path of moral responsibility entwined with social justice. Regardless of the ebbs and flows of societal tides, the Church steadfastly articulates a vision of humanity that is both revolutionary and immutable. The principle of human dignity, rooted in the Imago Dei—the image of God—reverberates through the corridors of ecclesial thought. This theological groundwork underpins the Church's mandate to champion the causes of the oppressed, the marginalized, and the disenfranchised.

Contemplating the notion of moral responsibility, one must wrestle with the age-old question: What does the Lord require of thee? The answer, as articulated within the Church's teachings, beckons a dual commitment to moral righteousness and the active pursuit of justice. The moral imperatives of the Church transcend individual piety and pour forth into the communal and societal realms, challenging the faithful to reflect Christ's luminous love in their interactions with the broader world. Hence, social justice does not merely emerge as a corollary of personal holiness; it is inherently interwoven with the very essence of Christian moral life.

One cannot overlook the ecclesiastical decrees pronounced in seminal documents, which like guiding stars, orient the Church toward a just society. The Encyclicals by successive Pontiffs, from 'Rerum Novarum' to 'Fratelli Tutti', elucidate with clarity the Church's unwavering solidarity with the poor and marginalized. These documents are not to be perceived as relics of doctrinal antiquity but as living testimonies to the Church's ongoing commitment to social transformation. They call upon each faithful soul to actively engage in the pursuit of a just order, where the rights and dignity of every individual are upheld and cherished.

Why does this preoccupation with social justice take center stage in the moral exegesis of the Church? Simply put, the Gospel of Christ is innately concerns itself with both the temporal and the eternal welfare of humanity. The teachings of Christ were inherently bound up with an advocacy for the downtrodden, evident in the Beatitudes where He proclaims blessings upon the poor, the meek, and those who hunger for righteousness. These are no mere poetic utterances; they are radical invitations to reconfigure societal norms based on divine love and justice.

Furthermore, divine law, by its very nature, necessitates an active engagement in rectifying social wrongs. The Ten Commandments extend beyond individual morality, demanding fidelity in social conduct and a profound respect for the communal welfare. The Catechism eloquently explicates this, forging a path that intertwines the personal and the communal, illuminating the inseparability of individual sanctity from social justice.

As we dwell upon the ethical implications of Church teachings, the exigency of moral responsibility becomes ever more palpable. The Church propounds that each faithful individual, imbued with the dignity of the divine image, is called to be a steward of justice. Bioethics, for instance, lays bare the existential questions surrounding the sanctity of life, urging the faithful to uphold human dignity at every stage, from conception to natural death. This theological stance intertwines seamlessly with social justice, emphasizing not just the preservation of life, but the enhancement of its quality for all individuals, especially the vulnerable and the oppressed.

One may ponder how this theological mandate translates into tangible action. Herein lies the Church's advocacy for policies that champion the common good. The preferential option for the poor, a cornerstone of Catholic social teaching, requires an unrelenting commitment to elevate the plight of the impoverished. This divine imperative compels the faithful to examine the structures of society critically, eradicating systems that perpetuate injustice and fostering those that advance equitable opportunities for all. This, indeed, is the heart of moral responsibility birthed from the Church's ethical teachings.

The interplay between social justice and moral responsibility also manifests in the ethos of subsidiarity. This principle underscores the importance of empowering individuals and communities to take action at the most immediate level, promoting participation and decentralization. It commits the faithful to engage in the societal healing process, ensuring that each person, regardless of their station in life, has the opportunity to contribute meaningfully to the common good. Such participatory justice is not merely an adjunct but a critical component of the Church's vision for a just society.

To elucidate further, the Church's role in social justice extends beyond the confines of doctrine into the corporeal world of activism. Historical contexts reveal that the Church has often stood as a bulwark against oppression, championing causes that protect the dignity and rights of individuals. This commitment continues in modern applications, where the Church and its adherents endeavor to ameliorate societal injustices through various forms of advocacy, ranging from grassroots movements to global outreach initiatives. This seamless integration of doctrine and action embodies the ethical implications of the Church's teachings on moral responsibility.

Thus, to grasp fully the Church's teachings on social justice and moral responsibility is to recognize an intricate web of divine love, unwavering justice, and human dignity. It challenges every Christian soul not only to live a life of moral integrity but to ardently pursue the establishment of a just society. The clarion call of the Church resonates through the ages, summoning the faithful to be the salt and light of the earth, embodying Christ's transformative love in a world marred by inequities. This, indeed, is the highest expression of the ethical implications of Church teachings— a symphony of divine grace and human endeavor.

Chapter 5: Apologetics for Human Dignity

In our epoch, where the sanctity of human life hath been oft assailed, it is imperative to mount a robust defense for the inherent dignity bestowed upon man by the Divine. Verily, this dignity stands not merely on frail human assertions, but is anchored in the unassailable truths of sacred Scriptures and the rational discernments of venerable theologians. Forsooth, to cognize human worth, one must traverse the fertile grounds of logic and revelation, wherein the very nature of man as imago Dei (the image of God) is illuminated. This chapter doth undertake the noble task of elucidating and defending this ineffable dignity, marshalling arguments both ancient and modern. Thus, we turn our gaze upon the rational and scriptural apologetics that fortify the impregnable citadel of human worth, countering every onslaught with reasoned rebuttals and enlightened exegesis, wielding our pens as swords in this most righteous endeavor.

Rational Defense of Human Dignity

To advance a rational defense of human dignity, one must navigate the confluence of reason, morality, and theological insight, for it is within this triad that the irrefutable worth of the human person is most cogently substantiated. Man is not a mere assemblage of flesh and bone, but a being imbued with an innate, inviolable sanctity, conferred by the Divine image. Reason supports this assertion, aligning itself with the natural law and the introspective certitude that humans possess an inherent value, unattached to utilitarian function. Moreover, the philosophical treatises of antiquity, expounded by the likes of Aristotle and the Stoics, reiterate the unique role of rational beings within the cosmos. Hence, to deny human dignity is to assault the very essence of rational discourse, moral order, and theological verity—it is to sever the Gordian knot that binds our understanding of existence, virtue, and purpose. Thus, the apologist, wielding the twin swords of faith and reason, stands resolute against the tides of skepticism, asserting that every human person, regardless of condition or circumstance, is worthy of profound respect and unwavering dignity.

Logical Arguments Supporting Dignity stand as pillars that elevate the intrinsic worth of the human person, fortified by reason and truth. In a realm where myriad voices clamor for dominion over the understanding of human value, it becomes ever more vital to anchor dignity in logic as immutable as it is profound.

Let us first consider the foundational argument rooted in human rationality. Distinct from other creatures, humanity is graced with the gift of reason. This faculty not only allows for self-reflection and learning but also for moral deliberation. The very capacity to engage in rational thought underscores our unique position in creation, positioning human dignity as an inherent reality rather than a contingent attribute.

The argument extends and reaches into the realm of natural law, a concept championed by both theologians and philosophers. According to natural law, certain rights and moral precepts are universally inscribed upon the hearts of men and women, discernible through the use of reason. This universal code, which predicates the equality of all persons, provides a reinforcing bastion for the notion that dignity is not a societal construct but a fundamental aspect of what it means to be human.

Another pillar supporting human dignity is the moral dimension of human actions, which demands accountability and virtue. If human acts were devoid of moral weight, considerations of dignity would be bereft of substance. The moral argument insists that the ability to discern and choose the good— an act of free will— places humanity in a sui generis position. This freedom of moral choice is inseparable from human dignity; without it, the concept loses its essence and becomes a hollow abstraction.

The principle of autonomy further enriches this discourse. Human autonomy—the capacity for self-governance and self-determination— is not merely a social convention but a natural right. Autonomy reflects our ability to chart the course of our lives, make decisions based on moral reasoning, and bear the consequences thereof. When societies or institutions infringe upon this autonomy, they undermine the very dignity intrinsic to the human person.

Furthermore, an argument for dignity rooted in the relational aspect of human existence must be illuminated. Man is not an island; our worth is unfurled in communion with others. This interconnectedness implies a reciprocal recognition of dignity— to acknowledge it in oneself is to acknowledge it in others, fostering a community wherein mutual respect is paramount. Absent such recognition, relationships deteriorate into power dynamics, obliterating the sanctity of human interaction.

From a metaphysical perspective, human dignity finds firm grounding in the notion of imago Dei, the belief that humanity is made in the image of God. This theological assertion, beyond its sacred resonance, offers a logical corollary: if one holds that a transcendent being imbues humanity with divine likeness, then the worth of a human is immeasurable and inviolable. Any assault on human dignity thus becomes an affront to the divine.

Moreover, the universe bears witness to the uniqueness of the human soul. In a cosmos teeming with life forms, it is humanity alone that contemplates its own existence, seeks meaning beyond mere survival, and aspires to transcendence. These qualities— self-awareness, pursuit of meaning, and transcendence— are attributes logically corollary to a dignified nature. A being capable of such contemplation demands a recognition of its inherent worth.

The philosophical tradition also offers substantial assistance through the principle of intentionality. Intentionality, the directedness of consciousness toward an object, underscores the reality that human minds are geared toward understanding and interacting with the world in meaningful ways. This directedness reflects an inherent order and purpose, again validating claims of intrinsic value and dignity. To deny dignity is to deny this intrinsic purpose, rendering human experience a mere accident devoid of value.

Analogously, the teleological argument strengthens our apologetics for human dignity. According to this line of reasoning, everything in creation has an end or purpose (telos). For humanity, the telos involves not only individual flourishing but also the cultivation of virtues and the fulfillment of one's moral and spiritual dimensions. If human beings possess such an ultimate purpose, it logically follows that their lives and choices hold intrinsic worth, attesting to their dignity.

In summary, the logical defense of human dignity is multi-faceted and robust. It encompasses the unique capacity for reason, the universal precepts of natural law, moral accountability, autonomy, relationality, theological insights, metaphysical considerations, philosophical principles, and teleological ends. Each thread weaves into a unifying tapestry that affirms the sacred and inviolable worth of every human person. To recognize this is to champion a truth as old as humanity itself, a verity that neither time nor tide can erode.

Counterarguments and Rebuttals within the broader discourse of a Rational Defense of Human Dignity necessitate rigorous examination, for it is in the dialectic clash of ideas that truth often emerges more luminously. The sanctity of human dignity, though profoundly rooted in theological, philosophical, and moral grounds, faces a multitude of counterarguments challenging its universality and applicability.

One prominent critique arises from the camp of radical individualism, which contends that human dignity, as framed by the Church, imposes external moral standards that restrict an individual's autonomy. They argue that dignity is self-determined and subjective, thus rejecting any universal claims. Such a perspective posits that the concept of dignity should adapt to personal choices, failing to recognize an absolute moral order.

In rebutting this position, one must assert that true human dignity, as envisioned by the Church, is not a mere subjective sentiment but an objective reality grounded in the imago Dei—the belief that humans are created in the image of God. Autonomy, while valuable, becomes genuinely meaningful only when exercised within the framework of moral truths that transcend personal whims. By aligning personal freedom with divine law, individuals possess the liberty to actualize their fullest potential, rather than succumbing to capricious desires.

Furthermore, another counterargument stems from utilitarian perspectives which claim that human dignity must yield to the greater good of society. Advocates of this view assert that individual rights and dignities may at times be justifiably compromised to achieve the greatest happiness for the greatest number. They might cite examples such as the allocation of limited medical resources or controversial bioethical practices to support their standpoint.

Against this, the rebuttal stands firm in the teachings of the Church which hold that the inviolability of human dignity must never be sacrificed at the altar of utilitarian calculus. The worth of a human person lies not in their utility but in their inherent value as bearers of divine likeness. The principle of the common good, central to Catholic thought, harmonizes communal welfare with the protection of individual dignity, refusing to endorse any action that degrades the inherent worth of even a single person.

Some argue from a materialistic and secular humanist perspective, which denies the existence of any spiritual dimension or divine image within humanity, contending that dignity is a social construct evolved for pragmatic reasons. This view reduces human worth to mere biological and sociological functions, denying any sacred or metaphysical element.

Rebutting the materialistic reductionism, one must elucidate how the Church's teaching on human dignity offers a more holistic understanding of the person—affirming not just our physical and social dimensions but also our spiritual and transcendental essence. This spiritual foundation provides a more robust and enduring basis for the respect of human dignity, transcending temporal social constructs and affirming an eternal truth about our nature.

Furthermore, the challenge arises from cultural relativists who claim that concepts of dignity vary across cultures and that no single definition holds universal applicability. They posit that what one tradition venerates as dignified, another may deem inconsequential or even offensive, thus challenging the universality of the Church's teaching.

In response, the rebuttal acknowledges cultural diversity while asserting the existence of universal moral principles applicable across all human societies. The concept of human dignity, although understood and expressed differently across cultures, ultimately points to a shared recognition of intrinsic human worth. The Church's teachings serve as a moral compass that respects cultural peculiarities while upholding a core set of values necessary for authentic human flourishing.

Some critics, particularly within scientific communities, argue against the notion of human dignity on the grounds that empirical evidence and evolutionary biology do not support any inherent moral status. They view humanity as a product of natural processes, with no intrinsic value that surpasses other forms of life.

In rebuttal to scientific reductionism, it is essential to recognize that the empirical sciences, while profoundly illuminating in many respects, are not equipped to address questions of metaphysical and moral significance. The worth of the human person cannot be fully comprehended through materialistic lenses alone. The Church's teaching on human dignity incorporates both reason and faith, offering a synthesis that respects scientific insights while transcending them to affirm a deeper spiritual truth.

Lastly, counterarguments also arise from within philosophical realms such as existential nihilism, which denies any inherent purpose or value to human existence. This perspective asserts that human dignity is an arbitrary construct in a universe devoid of meaning or value.

A rebuttal to existential nihilism must delve into the profound richness of Christian existential thought, which acknowledges the freedom and responsibility inherent in human existence while affirming an ultimate purpose and telos grounded in the divine. Human dignity, far from being arbitrary, is rooted in the objective truth of God's love and purpose for each individual, offering a hope and meaning that transcends human despair.

In summation, the rational defense of human dignity is fortified through robust rebuttals to these varied counterarguments. The interplay of theological, philosophical, and ethical responses constructs an unshakeable edifice that upholds the intrinsic worth of every person. While counterarguments challenge the universal applicability and objective reality of human dignity, the rebuttals grounded in Catholic teaching reveal a more profound truth that respects both the autonomy of individuals and the universal call to recognize and uphold the sanctity of human life.

Scriptural Apologetics

In crafting a bulwark of Scriptural Apologetics, one must dwell upon the sacred texts and discern therein the luminous threads that attest to man's inherent worth. The holy writ, both Old and New Testaments alike, doth weave an intricate tapestry of divine affirmation, portraying man as a creature fashioned in the very image of the Almighty. From the Genesis account where man is crafted from dust yet breathed into life by the Spirit of God, unto the Gospels where Christ's incarnation and sacrificial love extol the supreme value of each soul, the Scriptures offer a veritable cornucopia of evidence for human dignity. One must assert with unwavering conviction that the divine narrative itself forms an irrefutable apologetic, demonstrating that man's value is neither mere social construct nor philosophical conjecture, but an eternal verity proclaimed by the divine Logos. Thus, the Word of God remains the chief cornerstone upon which any defense of human dignity must rest, affording an unassailable foundation against which no temporal sophistry may stand.

Biblical Evidence for Human Worth can be traced through the annals of the Holy Scriptures, where the inherent dignity of the human person is woven into the very fabric of divine revelation. The testimony of sacred texts affirms the sacredness of human life from its creation in the imago Dei (image of God) to the messianic fulfillment in the New Testament, hence laying a formidable foundation for an apologetical defense of human dignity.

In the Book of Genesis, the primeval narrative elucidates that "God created man in his own image, in the image of God created he him; male and female created he them." (Genesis 1:27). Here lies a profound theological assertion: the human person, as a unique creation, embodies the divine likeness, imbuing each individual with an unassailable worth. The term 'image' here is not to be understood merely in a physical sense but rather as a representation of divine attributes: rationality, capacity for love, and dominion over creation.

This foundational doctrine is further echoed in the Psalms where King David marvels, "What is man, that thou art mindful of him? And the son of man, that thou visitest him? For thou hast made him a little lower than the angels, and hast crowned him with glory and honour." (Psalm 8:4-5). David's poetic meditation reveals a cosmic significance bestowed upon humanity, an ennoblement that surpasses all earthly creatures, draped in glory and honor. Such passages venerate the sanctity of human existence, propounding an exalted view that undergirds the concept of human dignity.

The prophetic literature also provides persuasive validation of the intrinsic worth of each person. From Isaiah's profound declaration (Isaiah 43:1) - "Fear not: for I have redeemed thee, I have called thee by thy name; thou art mine" - emerges an intimate portrait of divine-human relationship. In these words, the individuality and preciousness of each human soul are underlined, emphasizing a personal God who calls and redeems. This personal calling reflects a deliberate and intimate value placed on each human life.

Turning our gaze to the New Testament, the Incarnation stands as the cornerstone of human dignity. The Word becoming flesh (John 1:14) is the divine act that sanctifies human nature itself. In Christ, humanity is imbued with a dignity that is not merely intrinsic but is also relational - defined in terms of its relationship to the divine. The Incarnation signifies that human nature is assumed and elevated, a solid affirmation of mankind's worth.

Christ's teachings consistently reflect a deliberate elevation of the marginalized and the outcast, underscoring the universal worth of all individuals. "Inasmuch as ye have done it unto one of the least of these my brethren, ye have done it unto me." (Matthew 25:40). This radical identification of Christ with the 'least' imbues every human act of charity with a divine significance, reaffirming that dignity is not contingent upon social status but is an indelible mark upon every person. Thus, dignity is democratized to all facets of humanity.

Moreover, the Pauline epistles, with their theological profundity, further elucidate the Christian concept of human dignity. St. Paul, in 1 Corinthians 3:16, instructs the faithful, "Know ye not that ye are the temple of God, and that the Spirit of God dwelleth in you?" This theological insight presents the human body as a sacred vessel, a dwelling place of the Holy Spirit, and thereby calls for a respect and reverence for human life that transcends physical appearance or ability.

To unpack the comprehensive scriptural evidence for human worth requires not just intellectual assent but a recognition of the lived implications. Every scriptural narrative, every divine utterance, serves as an emblem of an undergirding theological anthropology that celebrates human dignity. This sacred demarcation impels moral theologians and sociologists alike to advocate and uphold the intrinsic worth of every person.

As we traverse the scriptural panorama, we observe a divine consistency in the portrayal of human worth. The various covenants – from Noah to Abraham, Moses, and finally the New Covenant in Christ – collectively underscore a relational dignity grounded in divine initiative and fidelity. Each covenantal relationship amplifies this worth, illustrating a continuum of divine-human interaction that underscores human dignity in temporal and eschatological dimensions.

It is, therefore, incumbent upon the apologist to wield this biblical evidence adeptly in the arena of moral theology. This is more than an abstract theological exercise; it is the lifeblood of a lived faith that seeks to manifest the love of Christ through justice, compassion, and respect for human dignity. By anchoring our apologetics in the rich soil of Scripture, we avail ourselves of a wellspring of divine truth that ardently defends the worth of each human person.

Responding to Common Objections forms a cornerstone within the vast discourse on the nature of human dignity, as espoused through sacred Scripture. The divine word, as transmitted through the holy pages of the Bible, stands as both sword and shield in the defense of the sanctity and worth of the human person. Yet, the echoes of dissent often resonate through the chambers of theological and moral discourse, presenting objections that demand a resolute and thoughtful response. Let us, then, wade into these murky waters and elucidate the verity and substance behind scriptural affirmations of human dignity.

First among the objections commonly raised is the perceived ambiguity or inconsistency within the Scriptures regarding the true worth of the human person. Critics posit that the Old Testament, with its myriad laws and occasional harsh decrees, portrays humanity in a manner that seems at odds with the notion of intrinsic dignity. Consider, for instance, the prescribed penalties in Levitical law for various transgressions, which some argue impose an overly punitive framework.

To address this contention, one must delve into the hermeneutic principle of progressive revelation. The strictures and ordinances of the Old Testament are part of a larger divine pedagogy, tailored to the spiritual and moral development of a nascent covenant community. These laws, while seemingly austere, ultimately aim to guide the Israelites towards a deeper understanding of holiness and justice. Moreover, amidst these laws, one finds resplendent affirmations of human dignity, such as the Imago Dei in Genesis, where humanity is created in the image and likeness of God. This profound declaration lays the foundational bedrock for all subsequent theological reflections on human worth.

Another prevalent objection arises from the New Testament's discussions of servitude, particularly the Pauline epistles which include exhortations for slaves to obey their masters. Skeptics argue that such passages endorse a diminished view of human autonomy and dignity, creating a stumbling block for contemporary adherents who seek to uphold the inviolable worth of every person.

This objection warrants a nuanced exegesis. The apostle Paul's writings must be contextualized within the socio-economic milieu of the Greco-Roman world, where slavery was an entrenched institution. Paul's exhortations, far from condoning the practice, seek to infuse it with Christian ethics, emphasizing mutual respect and the recognition of the slave as a brother in Christ. His epistle to Philemon, wherein he advocates for the emancipation of Onesimus, a runaway slave, is a testament to the transformative potential of the Gospel. By urging Philemon to receive Onesimus not merely as a servant but as a beloved brother, Paul underscores an egalitarian vision that transcends societal norms.

One must also reckon with the objection centered upon the perceived exclusivity and particularism of the Biblical narrative. Critics contend that the divine favor seemingly shown to Israel neglects the broader human family, thus undermining the universality of human dignity. This perception, however, is dispelled upon closer inspection of the scriptural canon.

The election of Israel, far from being an act of divine favoritism, serves a representative purpose within the divine economy. Israel is chosen to be a "light to the nations," exemplifying a covenantal relationship with God that is ultimately inclusive and not exclusive. The messianic prophecy, encapsulated in the Suffering Servant songs of Isaiah, heralds a time when all nations shall be gathered unto the Lord, thus affirming the universality of the human vocation and dignity.

Conversely, the New Testament reiterates and fulfills this promise of inclusivity. Christ's ministry, typified by his interactions with Samaritans, Gentiles, and societal outcasts, inaugurates a new covenant in which all are invited to partake of the divine life. The Pauline corpus, echoing this sentiment, proclaims, "There is neither Jew nor Greek, there is neither slave nor free, there is no male and female, for you are all one in Christ Jesus" (Gal. 3:28). Such pronouncements reinforce the scriptural testimony to the intrinsic worth and equality of every human being.

Critics also raise the issue of the problem of suffering and evil, questioning how Scripture can proclaim human dignity in the face of profound and pervasive suffering. This objection, deeply existential and poignant, probes the heart of the human experience and the divine narrative alike. Here, the Biblical response is neither simplistic nor dismissive but profoundly incarnational.

The Book of Job, considered a theological treatise on suffering, wrestles with these questions with raw honesty. Job's narrative does not offer pat answers; rather, it invites the sufferer into a posture of trust and dialogue with the Divine. The New Testament builds upon this, presenting the quintessential response to suffering in the person of Christ. The Incarnation itself is the ultimate affirmation of human dignity, wherein the Divine takes on the fragility of human flesh, walks among us, suffers with us, and redeems from within.

Finally, accusations of subjective ethical stances within Scripture pose another challenge to the perception of universal human dignity. The historical and cultural particularities of Scriptural texts, some argue, result in subjective moral imperatives that are not universally applicable. This critique often extends to perceived discrepancies between Scriptural moral teachings and modern ethical frameworks.

The hermeneutical key lies in discerning the timeless principles embedded within the cultural expressions. The moral kernel of Scriptural commandments—justice, mercy, love, and respect for the other—transcends cultural contingencies and speaks to the perennial human condition. The moral teachings of Scripture are not ensnared by temporal norms but offer guiding principles adaptable to various contexts. Herein lies the wisdom and enduring applicability of Biblical ethics, a robust framework capable of informing and enriching contemporary moral discourse.

In summation, the manifold objections posed to the scriptural foundation of human dignity, when carefully scrutinized and contextually interpreted, reveal the profound coherence and enduring truth of the divine word. Scripture, far from being an antiquated relic, continues to speak with authority and relevance to the intrinsic worth and dignity of the human person. Thus, through diligent study and faithful exegesis, the faithful apologist can confidently address and dispel these objections, reaffirming the Church's unwavering commitment to upholding the sanctity of every human life.

Chapter 6: The Relationship Between Dignity and Life

In the inexorable dance of existence, where flesh meets spirit and time unravels its threads, we find the sanctity of life and dignity forever intertwined. Herein lies a profound symbiosis: life, in its inception and culmination, cradles the innate dignity bestowed by our Creator. The Church, a custodian of this sacred interplay, proclaims that from the nascent heartbeat of the unborn to the twilight years of the aged, each moment is imbued with divine worth. Thus, the moral edifice upon which our doctrines stand does more than merely affirm life; it venerates it. To violate the sanctity of life at any stage—be it through abortion, euthanasia, or neglect of the vulnerable—becomes not only an affront to existence but a betrayal of inherent dignity. In these temporal vessels, fragile though they may appear, resides an eternal glory that commands respect, compassion, and unwavering moral commitment.

Ethical Dimensions of Human Life

In the grand tapestry that is life, woven with threads of moral fabric, we discern the profound confluence of ethics and human dignity. Each soul, an echo of the Divine, presents not merely a vessel of existence but a beacon of inherent worth. The ethical dimensions encircle the essence of our being with questions that pierce through the mundane into the celestial, demanding us to reckon with the immutable value of every life. Herein lies the sublime interplay between moral considerations and the sanctity of life itself, as ordained by the teachings of the Holy Church. To thread upon paths of morality is to affirm the dignity imbued within us by the Creator, a dignity not subject to the vicissitudes of time or circumstance. Each action, then, becomes a testament to our reverence for this sacred endowment, seeking always to mirror the divine love that has carved our very nature. In this pursuit, life is elevated to a sacrament, imbued with ethical significance that transcends the banality of temporal existence, anchoring us firmly in the eternal truths of our faith.

Church Teachings on Abortion are deeply interwoven within the broader tapestry of the Church's stance on the dignity of human life. The ethos that crowns every human being with intrinsic worth originates from the divine essence that, according to the sacred doctrine, imparts life. Ergo, the ethical dimensions of human life are inviolable, encompassing the nascent stages of existence, specifically the unborn.

From the moment of conception, the Church asserts that a unique and unrepeatable human life begins, imbued with a soul, thus demanding the utmost respect and protection. The teachings stem from the belief that life is a gift from God, woven with purpose and dignity. In this light, abortion is not merely a medical or social issue, but a profound moral concern.

The sanctity of life, as elucidated by magisterial documents and the unbroken tradition of the Church, confers an immutable dignity upon the unborn. Prominent encyclicals like "Evangelium Vitae" by Pope John Paul II vehemently defend this premise, affirming the Church's unwavering stance against abortion. The document declares, "Human life is sacred and inviolable at every moment of existence, including the initial phase which precedes birth." This grandeur of human life offers no latitude for termination, regardless of circumstances, save for the preservation of another life at risk.

Within the context of the "Ethical Dimensions of Human Life," the condemnation of abortion is grounded in a theology that sees every human being as created in the Imago Dei, the image of God. This foundational belief elevates the debate beyond social or individual autonomy to a divine mandate. Even amidst a culture that may posit conflicting views on personal liberty, the Church remains steadfast, with teachings anchored in divine revelation and natural law.

Furthermore, abortion is depicted as a grave moral disorder, one that not only transgresses divine law but also disrupts the natural order ordained by the Creator. It is an affront to the innate dignity that every human holds by virtue of their creation. Hence, the Church calls for the protection of vulnerable lives within the womb, akin to the protection mandated for all human beings.

While illustrative of high moral principles, the Church's stance is not devoid of compassion or understanding of human frailty. Pastoral care and support for those facing the trials of unplanned pregnancies are vigorously promoted. Church teachings emphasize the importance of offering love, counsel, and practical assistance to mothers in distress, thereby upholding the dignity of both mother and child.

The ethical dimension further encompasses the ramifications that abortion has on the fabric of society. Abortion, viewed through the ecclesiastical lens, truncates the continuity of life and negates potential contributions to the human community. By terminating a nascent life, the act forecloses the future flourishing of an individual destined to partake in God's grand design. Thus, the Church's teaching posits abortion as an impediment to societal progress rooted in the harmonious development of every individual.

Moreover, the Church advocates for a culture of life, promoting alternatives to abortion such as adoption, and fostering a societal environment where children are welcomed and valued. It calls upon the faithful to engage in acts that affirm life, show solidarity with those in crisis, and work towards societal structures that support life-affirming choices.

The condemnation of abortion is interspersed with affirmations of mercy and forgiveness. The sacrament of reconciliation offers hope and healing for those who have partaken in abortion, underscoring the redemptive aspect of Church teaching. The ethos here is not solely punitive, but restorative, inviting transgressors to embrace divine mercy and regain their dignity.

Consequently, Church teachings on abortion are not an isolated doctrine but resonate with a comprehensive theology that integrates the respect for human life at all stages. This doctrine extends its defenses to the unborn with the same fervor as it protects the elderly, the infirm, and the marginalized. The universal principle is a testament to the Church's unwavering dedication to upholding human dignity in its entirety.

In summation, the Church's teachings on abortion reveal a profound commitment to upholding the sanctity and dignity of human life. These teachings stand as a bulwark against any act that would devalue or destroy nascent life, resonating with the divine command to cherish and protect all human beings. In this regard, the ethical dimensions of human life, shaped by these teachings, are illuminated and safeguarded, reflecting the Church's unwavering commitment to the dignity of the human person.

Euthanasia and the Sanctity of Life finds itself nestled within the heart of the ethical dimensions of human life, where it grapples with profound questions: What constitutes a dignified existence? Can a life, deemed by some as burdened with suffering, ever be sanctioned to its premature conclusion? The luminous ballast of the Catholic faith offers a steadfast compass pointing to an unwavering respect for life's inviolability.

The sanctity of life embodies a perennial doctrine of the Church, a divine echo that reverberates through the annals of theological and philosophical inquiry. In the face of contemporary appeals to euthanasia, one is beckoned to remember that life itself is an irreplaceable gift from the Creator. This divine endowment is inscribed with an inherent dignity, unassailable by the mere vicissitudes of human suffering and uncertainty.

In this regard, the Church's stance is unequivocal. Euthanasia, defined as an act or omission which intentionally causes death, so as to eliminate suffering, is firmly repudiated. According to the Congregation for the Doctrine of the Faith, such an act is a grave violation of the law of God, as it is the deliberate and morally unacceptable killing of a human person.

While the dawn of the modern era has seen humanity wrestle with unprecedented medical advancements and ethical dilemmas, the invocation of euthanasia as compassionate relief does not find sanctuary within the framework of Catholic moral teaching. The Church's moral teachings underscore that suffering, though arduous and often incomprehensible, possesses the capacity for profound sanctification. In the crucible of suffering, an individual may find a renewed closeness to Christ, who Himself knew the pangs of human agony.

To the Roman Catholic, to the theologian who contemplatively weighs the scales of ethics, and to the vigilant sociologist, the rhetoric of a "death with dignity" must be carefully parsed. For dignity, couched in the divine regard for each soul, is not diminished by suffering or infirmity. True dignity, as espoused by Catholic teaching, is interwoven with the mysterious yet immutable value of each life, created imago Dei— in the image of God.

Indeed, the argument extends beyond theological assertion to touch upon the very roots of societal ethos. The legal and social acceptance of euthanasia could precipitate a perilous path, eroding the moral fabric and devaluing human life at its most vulnerable. The elderly, the disabled, and the terminally ill require not an escape through euthanasia but the embrace of a society that recognizes their unalterable worth.

Understanding and compassion must, therefore, translate into endeavors that facilitate true healing: palliative care, emotional support, spiritual guidance, and, above all, a recognition of the sanctity inherent in every stage of human existence. It is through such avenues that the genuine dignity of the human person is preserved, revering the life given by the Maker.

In juxtaposing the philosophical musings of antiquity, the Church Fathers such as Augustine and Aquinas have provided a perennial wisdom. Augustine, with his deliberations on human nature, encapsulates the tension of suffering and divine providence. Aquinas affords us the concept of the sacred person, attributing to each life an inalienable worth that resists any attempt to terminate it prematurely.

One must bear in mind, the sacramental vision of life offered by the Church. Baptism, Eucharist, and Anointing of the Sick expound a sacred narrative where every life, irrespective of its temporal suffering, is tethered to an eternal destiny. Hence, any endorsement of euthanasia starkly juxtaposes this sacramental tapestry.

The ethical implication transcends the realm of individual choice, touching upon the communal and cosmic order. As the Church echoes in her pastoral care, the measure of a society can be discerned in how it treats its weakest members. This ethos demands a robust defense against the encroachments of euthanasia, reaffirming life's sanctity at every juncture.

Let it not be forgotten that within the folds of the Church, there is an abundant reservoir of pastoral and spiritual resources. Those grappling with terminal illnesses and their loved ones are invited into a community that marches together on the pilgrimage of life, one that neither romanticizes suffering nor opts for its gravest escape. Rather, it is in the very endurance of suffering where solidarity with the Crucified Christ remains profound.

Ultimately, the question of euthanasia and the sanctity of life finds its zenith in the face of Christ. His passion and resurrection cast light upon the darkest dimensions of human suffering, revealing a dignity unseverable by death. To embrace this perspective is to embrace a hope firmly anchored in an eternal vision of life, where temporal afflictions are transformed, rather than truncated.

dignity in various stages of life

From the nascent breath of life, as the babe doth stir in the womb, till the twilight of existence as the aged soul readies for eternity, dignity's hallowed essence remains steadfast. Not merely a birthright endowed at the start, but a sacred continuum graced by divine imprint; in each season's passage, a reflection of divine grandeur. The feeble infant, the blooming youth, the stalwart adult, and the venerable elder—each bears a visage of the Creator's masterpiece. Thus, in all life's epochs, dignity ought resolutely be revered, a testament to the sanctity interwoven within our mortal journey, echoing the Church's sacred teachings and calling forth a reverence that spans the cradle to the grave.

The Elderly and the Vulnerable Amidst the grand arc of human existence, there resounds an inviolable obligation to uphold the dignity of every person, especially those who reside in the delicate valleys of life's later stages and in the crucible of vulnerability. In this exploration, we affirm an apologetic stance that champions the Church's moral teachings, which assert that the worth of an individual does not wither with age nor diminishes under the weight of frailty.

Our philosophical pilgrimage brings us to the heart of the matter, where one finds that human dignity is neither a vestment donned nor discarded by the seasons of life. Indeed, the words of Augustine remind us of the intrinsic worth encoded into our very being. "We are made in God's image," he declares, underscoring a truth that girds the Church's teachings —that dignity is innate and immutable, transcending the transitory afflictions of age and circumstance.

As we venture through the corridors of theological thought, Aquinas' Sanctus Persona resounds as a clarion call, bidding us to recognize the sacredness in every person. The grand tapestry of life unfolds, revealing the elderly as integral threads woven with divine purpose and deserving of veneration. Their years are not simply time accrued but wisdom accumulated, forming a bulwark of communal memory and traditions that anchor society in a continuum of faith and values.

In the solemn passages of papal encyclicals and conciliar documents, the Church speaks with unequivocal clarity. The voice of Vatican II echoes, enshrining the principle that respect for human dignity obligates us to safeguard the interests and well-being of the elderly and the vulnerable. It exhorts us to provide not merely the succor of material needs but to envelop them in a mantle of empathy and love.

One must not overlook the contemporary ethical milieu in which this discourse is enmeshed. The modern ethos often prizes utility and productivity, casting aside those deemed no longer contributory. This utilitarian calculus stands in stark contradistinction to the Church's vision that sees value in every breath, every beat of the heart, regardless of its vigor or frailty. Here, the moral theologian finds a battlefield of ideas, where the defense of human dignity must take precedence over the pragmatic exigencies of an efficiency-driven society.

In the praxis of these ethical principles, concrete actions are demanded. It is not enough to proffer entreaties and declarations; the embodiment of these ideals must manifest in our institutions and policies. The Church, through its manifold ministries, provides a beacon of hope and sanctuary, bearing witness to the truth that the elderly are treasures, repositories of life-long experiences and divine favor.

Yet, even as we champion these truths, we encounter the specter of suffering, which often envelops the vulnerable. This suffering, however, is not without purpose or meaning. The writings of Dostoevsky teach us that in suffering, there exists a transcendent possibility—a refinement of the spirit, a deepened communion with the Divine. Thus, the Church's mission is twofold: to alleviate suffering where possible and to provide meaning and companionship where it persists.

In the twilight of life, many find themselves beset by the isolations of age, physically and emotionally distant from the communities they once helped to build. Here, the principle of solidarity illuminates our path. It is incumbent upon families, parishes, and society at large to ensure that the elderly are not relegated to the peripheries but are drawn into the heart of communal and liturgical life. This enkindles not just their dignity, but enriches the entirety of the Christian community.

Furthermore, the vulnerable often include those whose voices are muffled by the margins of society—persons with disabilities, the impoverished, and those battling chronic illness. Their plight calls forth a commitment to social justice, rooted in the preferential option for the poor as articulated by Catholic Social Teaching. They are not mere recipients of charity but are co-participants in the community, bringing unique gifts and perspectives that enrich the whole.

The annals of history, sacred and secular alike, attest to the salvation wrought by revering those in the dusk of life. Consider the testimonies of the ancients who, even in pagan societies, revered their elders as sages. These echoes find fulfillment in the Christian dispensation where Christ

Himself became the paradigmatic Shepherd, seeking the marginalized and the weak.

Lastly, let us turn to the practical, where theological reflection meets the tangible world. It is imperative that public policies reflect the sanctity and dignity bestowed upon the elderly and the vulnerable. In healthcare, in housing, and in the justice system, the Church advocates for measures that not only protect but elevate the conditions of these beloved communities, ensuring they live not merely in want, but in dignity and peace.

It is here, at the intersection of dignity and life, that we offer our collective endeavor—a conscious reflection, a spirited defense, and an unwavering commitment to the sanctity of every human person. From the first breath to the final whisper, and in every moment of vulnerability, the Church stands as a testament to the eternal worth bestowed by the Creator upon each soul.

The Unborn and Infants doth present us with the profound and delicate task of establishing the intrinsic worth of those who dwell at the very edge of life. Brought into this world yet unseen, or merely in the early bloom of existence, they beckon consideration in the discourse on human dignity. Yea, let us not ignore their silent cry for respect and recognition.

Behold, in the encumbered beginning of a human life lies the essence of dignity, an aspect untarnished by age, achievements, or societal contributions. The Church, in her eternal wisdom, proclaims that from conception unto infancy, every creature begotten by God is deserving of unswerving reverence. Thus, the unborn in the womb holds equivalence in sanctity to the sage nearing dusk. Consider the divine proclamation in the Psalms: "For thou didst form my inward parts; thou didst knit me together in my mother's womb" (Psalm 139:13). Truly, does this not declare the unborn as a masterpiece awaiting to unfold?

We must glean from the scriptural truths that even the merest spark of life merits a temple of dignity. From the instant a heart begins to beat in cadence with the cosmos, there breathes a being woven with purpose and value. The Church persists in this teaching, despite the manifold challenges presented by modern ethos that would question the sanctity of nascent existence. Shall we not embrace our sacred duty to protect and honor these delicate lives?

Moreover, let us turn to the testimonies of venerable theologians who have pondered deeply on the nature of early life. Augustine, in his contemplations on human nature, asserts that all human beings bear the imago Dei – the image of God. In this light, the unborn and infants, though unpolished by earthly experiences, still radiate divine light. Can we then dismiss their worth by the simplistic measure of maturity? Nay, for their very being speaks of a higher order.

Thomas Aquinas contributes a compelling perspective by accentuating the soul's essence from the moment of conception. He argues, by the synergy of reason and faith, that the soul is infused at conception, creating a union so profound that its dignity transcends temporal age. Yea, this is an affirmation that every infant, from the first stirrings in the womb to their early cries, is enshrined with an inherent sanctity.

Let us not neglect the gravity of the Church's stance against abortion. Firmly rooted in the conviction that life begins at conception, the Church's moral teachings profess that any act to terminate an unborn life grieveth the divine order. This stance is a testament to the Church's unwavering acknowledgment of the unborn's dignity, requiring us to engage actively in the protection and nurture of nascent life.

Beyond theological assertions, we ought to reflect on the societal implications of valuing the lives of the unborn and infants. In recognizing their inherent dignity, we set the foundation for a society that values each human being from their inception to their final breath. Indeed, much can be garnered from a culture that strives to protect its youngest and most vulnerable. It cultivates an environment wherein compassion and respect flourish, benefitting all stages of life.

One may not overlook the role of parents and caregivers in enveloping infants and unborn children with dignity. By nurturing these tender lives, they act as stewards of God's creation, embracing the sacred duty to shepherd these souls. The Church, in turn, provides guidance and support, urging parents to recognize and cultivate the inherent worth of their children. This collaboration enriches the family as the domestic church, perpetuating the cycle of dignity and sanctity.

From this standpoint, the community is called to a collective responsibility. Societal structures and institutions must align themselves with the principles that uphold the worth of the unborn and infants. Policies and social services must be configured to support expectant mothers, provide adequate healthcare, and foster environments where every child is nurtured and valued.

To comprehend the fullness of dignity in the unborn and infants, one must also delve into the realm of bioethics. The Church, through her teachings, delineates that human dignity transcends mere biological processes. It is a mark of divine ordination, compelling us to navigate bioethical dilemmas with a compass grounded in moral values and respect for life.

Consider the advent of medical technologies that now allow us to peer into the womb, witnessing the earliest stages of life. These advancements, while profound, also bring forth moral responsibilities. The insights gained from such technologies should only reinforce our commitment to protect and honor life at its most vulnerable. They ought to caution us against the utilitarian impulses that may seek to commodify or diminish the sanctity of early existence.

Furthermore, reflect upon the communal and ecclesiastical responsibilities in preserving the dignity of the unborn and infants. The Church's mission is to bear witness to the truth of human dignity at every turn, advocating for the defenseless and voiceless. In this endeavor, clergy, religious, and laity alike must work in unison to create a culture where every child's life is affirmed and celebrated.

The interplay between faith and reason must also be navigated with care in this context. The objective truth of human dignity, as recognized by the Church, finds resonance in the natural law discernible by human reason. This synthesis empowers us to make a reasoned defense of the unborn and infants' dignity, not merely through theological constructs but through universally accessible arguments.

In conclusion, "The Unborn and Infants" stand as a testament to the sanctity that envelops life from its inception. The Church, in her wisdom and compassion, calls for the protection and reverence of these tender lives, challenging contemporary mores that would seek to marginalize them. By upholding the dignity of the unborn and infants, we reassert the fundamental truth that every life is a divine gift, deserving of honor and care.

Chapter 7: Social Justice and Human Dignity

Verily, the celestial interplay between social justice and human dignity standeth as the cornerstone of holy ethos in a morally vacillating world. As the Church's eternal compass guides us towards righteousness, we are beckoned to champion the inalienable worth of each soul. In the labyrinth of earthly dominions, wherein inequities lay heavy burdens upon the lowly and humility shines amidst grandeur, the clarion call of justice ringeth true. Central to the Catholic lexicon, the preferential option for the poor and the principles of solidarity and subsidiarity doth illuminate our path, urging faithful stewards to uplift the downtrodden. Thus, through the panoramic lens of history and in the present crucible of modernity, the Church, in her divine sagacity, embarks on a mission of merciful advocacy, heralding the sanctity of human life against the intricate tapestry of societal maladies.

Principles of Catholic Social Teaching

In the rich tapestry of Catholic moral doctrine, the "Principles of Catholic Social Teaching" stand as luminous beacons guiding the faithful towards a life that upholds and venerates the sanctity of the human person. These principles, rooted in the great tradition of the Church, call upon every soul to engage in actions that reflect justice and compassion. They urge us to recognize the inherent dignity bestowed upon every individual by virtue of being created in the image of the Almighty. The principles encompass the pursuit of the common good, the virtue of solidarity, and the necessity of subsidiarity, whereby each member of society bears a mutual responsibility to foster conditions wherein all may flourish. These tenets compel us to champion the cause of the marginalized and to ensure that the preferential option for the poor is not merely a saying, but a lived reality. Indeed, the principles serve as both a compass and a clarion call, directing the Church's moral mission in a world that often strays from the path of righteousness and equity.

Preferential Option for the Poor unfolds within the vast canopy of *Social Justice and Human Dignity*, illuminating a pathway that scintillates with the deep, ancient wisdom of *Principles of Catholic Social Teaching.* One must ponder with solemnity; the pivotal emphasis the Church places upon the impoverished is neither a casual directive nor a modern invention, but rather a beacon of moral clarity deeply entrenched in our spiritual and theological genesis. The roots of this doctrine can be seen intertwining through the annals of sacred scripture and ecclesiastical tradition, beckoning all humanity towards a higher plane of communal responsibility and sanctity.

Verily, the concept of a preferential option for the poor is not a mere footnote in the Church's magisterium but rather an echo reverberating through the divine ordination of justice and mercy. The Scriptural foundations beckon back to the Old Testament, where a cadence of divine injunctions commands the faithful to care for the orphan, the widow, and the stranger. Traversing further, the blessed Beatitudes resonant within the New Testament herald blessings upon the poor in spirit, for theirs is the kingdom of heaven. The ceaseless undercurrent of this teaching is a clarion call to elevate the downtrodden and marginalized as integral facets of the Church's mission.

What dost thou find in the Gospel's labyrinth if not an eternal testament of Christ's allegiance to the impoverished? His ministry was replete with acts of kindness towards the underprivileged, reaffirming their indispensable worth in the eyes of God. The incarnate Word, who had not a place to lay His head, unveiled the divine countenance most vividly among the lowliest, and in His gaze upon their suffering, we glimpse the grandeur of a cosmic compassion unbeheld by the unreflective eye.

Central to the principle of the preferential option is an assertion that poverty is not just an economic condition but a multifaceted despair implicating social exclusion, moral destitution, and spiritual despondency. The Church, acknowledging this, extends her arms in a sacrificial embrace, vowing to become a balm unto the wounds of the forsaken. Indeed the commitment to the poor is a litmus test, a measure, if you will, of the Church's fidelity to Christ Himself.

Let us delve into the intricate tapestry woven by the Fathers of our ecclesiastical tradition. Augustine, in his apostolic fervor, drew parallels between loving the least among us and loving Christ. "For he who loveth none but himself must surely delve into abyssal loneliness," Augustine opined, pleading that charity towards the destitute was the very essence of divine love incarnate. Thomas Aquinas, in his sublime treatises, enunciated that the stewardship of wealth is an obligation underpinned by justice, not merely benevolence. For, as Aquinas articulated with sagacious clarity, the superabundance held by one cannot be justified when another languishes in deprivation.

As one meanders through the history of ecclesiastical decrees, from Vatican II's emphatic engagements to the eloquent yet firm declarations of recent papal encyclicals, one finds a constancy in the appeal to uplift the impoverished. The Church's preferential option for the poor transcends the dichotomy of charity and justice, stitching them together into a singular fabric of moral imperatives that demand systemic change and personal virtue.

Systematic, structural advocacy for the rights and dignity of the impoverished is paramount. The Church's voice thus rings out from the wilderness of indifference, and echoing through hallowed sanctuaries, it proclaims that any society which marginalizes the poor repudiates its own humanity. This proclamation is not mere platitude but imbued with actionable wisdom. Policy prescriptions, ethical exhortations, and communal engagements all streamline into a cohesive action plan urging both institution and individual alike to undertake transformative justice.

Moreover, the Church envisages a reciprocity between the giver and the receiver; the act of aiding the poor is not unidirectional but a spiritual symbiosis enriching all parties. As we uplift the downtrodden, our own souls are refined and graced by divine favor. This reciprocal enrichment holds a mirror to the divine economy, where acts of mercy are celestial currency, yielding rewards far surpassing transient material gain.

Understanding this, it's imperative to look upon the persona of the poor not as mere objects of charity but as essential subjects of our shared humanity. The poor are the sacred vessels bearing the imago Dei, deserving of respect, love, and dignity in all facets of life. Indeed, to uplift the poor is to uphold the sanctity of the human person, a truth resounding with immutable clarity throughout the Church's doctrinal corpus.

Jerome's words serve as an emblematic reminder: "May the poor be as our masters, who present us with the keys to the kingdom." His exhortation captures the quintessence of the preferential option for the poor – an option not fashioned by human hands but ordained by divine wisdom, exhorting all humanity towards a more illuminated path of justice.

In summation, the preferential option for the poor, as anchored in the *Principles of Catholic Social Teaching,* is more than an ecclesiastical mandate; it is an invitation to partake in the divine act of restoration. In uniting ourselves with the plight of the impoverished, we not only affirm their dignity but also reclaim our own, for in the divine tapestry, each thread is integral to the whole. Let us, therefore, with unwavering conviction and inexorable zeal, heed this divine call to manifest the luminous brilliance of God's boundless love through our own acts of justice and charity towards the least of our brethren.

Solidarity and Subsidiarity are twin pillars that stand as sentinels over the vast expanse of Catholic Social Teaching, each holding aloft the sacred torch of human dignity and social justice. Just as a delicate balance in nature preserves the harmony of life, so too do these principles preserve the moral order, guiding the faithful in the intricate dance between communal support and individual autonomy.

At the heart of solidarity lies the recognition of our shared humanity. It is a clarion call, resonating through time and space, urging us to acknowledge that we are incontrovertibly bound to one another in the tapestry of existence. This interconnectedness impels us to transcend self-interest and extend our hands in genuine fraternity, fostering a community where the joys and sufferings of one become the joys and sufferings of all. It is both a virtue and an obligation, compelling Christians to stand in unwavering support of their neighbors, near and far.

One must never view solidarity as mere sentimentality or a vague ideal. It is, verily, a call to action, demanding tangible expressions of love and justice. By feeding the hungry, clothing the naked, and sheltering the homeless, we incarnate the Gospel's teachings and reflect the very essence of Christ's ministry on earth. Such acts of charity, though meritorious, aim to achieve something more profound—a world where justice prevails, and every soul is afforded the dignity inherent in God's creation.

Contrasted with solidarity, yet in harmonious complement, stands the principle of subsidiarity. It advocates that human affairs should be handled at the most immediate level consistent with their resolution. The wisdom in this principle is manifold, for it respects the individual's capacity for self-governance while cautioning against the perils of overreaching authority. By ensuring that decisions are made as close to the affected individuals as possible, subsidiarity preserves personal autonomy and promotes active participation in societal governance.

Subsidiarity prevents both the stifling paternalism of centralized power and the fragmentation that can result from uncoordinated local actions. It wisely discerns that higher orders of society must support, rather than supplant, the functions and responsibilities of lesser social bodies. Thus, the family, as the fundamental unit of society, is revered, with its sanctity protected from undue interference by external authorities.

Envisage a majestic oak tree, its roots profoundly entrenched in the fertile soil, providing life and stability to the towering structure above. Solidarity is akin to the intertwining roots that nourish and bind the community together, while subsidiarity reflects the sturdy trunk and branches that decentralize the nourishment, allowing each leaf and twig to flourish in its place. Combined, they form a robust and thriving organism, reminiscent of a just and participatory society.

In the application of solidarity and subsidiarity, the Catholic Church provides a beacon of hope. Through its teachings and actions, the Church endeavors to create a world where each person can thrive according to their God-given potential. It recognizes the unique gifts and responsibilities of every individual, community, and institution, promoting a synergy that is essential for integral human development.

The principle of solidarity brings into sharp focus our moral responsibility towards those who are marginalized and oppressed. It challenges us to confront systems of injustice and inequality that strip individuals of their dignity. By uniting our efforts in advocating for the poor, the disenfranchised, and the vulnerable, we knit a society that upholds the value of every human life.

Conversely, subsidiarity admonishes us to empower local communities and individuals with the autonomy to manage their own affairs. It affirms the wisdom and resourcefulness inherent at the grassroots level, encouraging self-reliance, innovation, and a sense of ownership in social and economic initiatives. It is a bulwark against the potential tyranny of distant bureaucracies and impersonal institutions.

Solidarity and subsidiarity, therefore, do not exist in isolation but operate in a delicate, interdependent balance. They call upon all members of society—from humble laypersons to ecclesiastical authorities and civic leaders—to recognize and fulfill their respective roles in building a just and compassionate world. Together, these principles illuminate a path that respects both communal interdependence and individual dignity, embodying the harmonious vision of Catholic social thought.

As we journey through the labyrinthine corridors of modern society, fraught with complex social, economic, and political challenges, the teachings of solidarity and subsidiarity remain ever-relevant. They guide us not only in our individual actions but also in the collective endeavor to craft policies and institutions that reflect the inherent worth of every person. Implementing these principles requires discernment, courage, and a steadfast commitment to the common good.

The ills of contemporary society, from rampant inequality to social fragmentation, are antidoted by solidarity and subsidiarity. These principles compel us to act justly, love tenderly, and walk humbly with our God, as the Prophet Micah exhorts. By doing so, we transform societies marred by division and strife into communities that echo the love and unity of the Divine Trinity.

In summation, **Solidarity and Subsidiarity** constitute the bedrock upon which Catholic Social Teaching rests, providing a framework for understanding and addressing the myriad issues confronting humanity. They encompass a dual mandate: to care for one another as brothers and sisters and to respect the autonomy and agency of individuals and local communities. By faithfully adhering to these principles, we uphold the dignity of the human person and advance the cause of social justice, leaving an indelible mark on the annals of moral and ethical thought.

The Role of the Church in Social Justice

In the grand tapestry of human society, wherein the threads of justice and dignity are oft interwoven, the Church stands as both weaver and guardian, stewarding the divine mandate to defend the least of our brethren. Through the annals of time, the Church has been an unwavering beacon, casting its light upon the downtrodden and marginalized, imbuing them with a voice that echoes the sanctity of human life. Its role hath not been merely passive, but rather an active force, grappling with the temporal powers to advocate for the sacred bond that ties all to their Creator. From the medieval almsgiving practices to modern advocacies exemplified in liberation theology and the social encyclicals, the Church's hand is ever extended, beckoning all toward a harmonious realm where equity and dignity prevail. Henceforth, it is not mere rhetoric but divine vocation that compels the Church to champion the cause of the meek, weaving justice into the very fabric of human existence, ensuring that the visage of divinity in each soul is both recognized and revered.

Historical Context and Modern Applications The manifold intricacies of social justice, entwined with the timeless notion of human dignity, have, through the ages, been profoundly influenced by the Church. From the earliest days of Christian doctrine to our present era, the Church has championed the cause of the downtrodden, invoking the sacred call for justice embedded in divine scripture.

Within the corridors of history, the Church, though not without blemish, has been a steadfast advocate for the marginalized. The nascent days of Christianity saw early disciples heed the exhortations of Christ Himself, rendering unto the impoverished what was inherently due. This divine mandate found expression in communal living, as depicted in the Acts of the Apostles, wherein the early Christians shared their possessions, ensuring that none among them suffered deprivation.

Moreover, the medieval period bore witness to the marvelous endeavors of monastic communities. Monasteries, becoming epicenters of learning and charity, extended their hands to poor farmers, providing sustenance and education. Figures like St. Francis of Assisi epitomized the very essence of this mission, forsaking worldly opulence to live alongside the destitute, embodying the principle of solidarity. Indeed, the Franciscan Order's works in feeding the hungry and clothing the naked stand as a testament to the Church's commitment to social justice.

In the throes of the industrial revolution, a time replete with economic upheaval and labor exploitation, the Church's voice did not waver. Prominent was Pope Leo XIII's *Rerum Novarum* of 1891, a seminal document underscoring the rights and dignity of workers. Herein, the Church condemned unbridled capitalism and pronounced a clarion call for the establishment of just wages and the formation of labor unions. Hence, the principles enunciated reverberated through the annals of history, invoking changes enduring to this day.

As the modern era dawned, the Church's social teaching evolved, yet its core remained immutable. The Second Vatican Council, most notably through the pastoral constitution *Gaudium et Spes*, articulated the human person's inherent dignity, emphasizing the Church's role in socio-economic matters. This period saw an intensified focus on the preferential option for the poor, urging the faithful to align their hearts and actions with the plights of those less fortunate. Thus, the Council reaffirmed, in no uncertain terms, the Church's unyielding commitment to justice.

Simultaneously, the prophetic voices of modern saints and leaders echoed these ages-old principles. Figures such as St. Óscar Romero in El Salvador and Mother Teresa of Calcutta advanced the cause of justice under the harshest of conditions. Their lives exemplify the moral teachings of the Church, becoming beacons of hope and instruments of divine mercy in a fractured world.

In our contemporary epoch, the Church's engagement in social justice manifests in both doctrine and practice. Charitable organizations, Catholic Relief Services among them, extend aid internationally, embodying the tenets of solidarity and subsidiarity. The Church's global network works tirelessly to combat poverty, injustice, and discrimination, aiming to restore dignity to all peoples.

One cannot overlook the Church's advocacy against modern-day evils such as human trafficking and systemic racism. Pope Francis has been particularly vociferous in addressing these issues, urging the faithful to fight against structures of sin that undermine human dignity. His encyclicals, including *Laudato Si'* and *Fratelli Tutti*, offer a blueprint for addressing ecological and social injustices, emphasizing a holistic approach to human and environmental well-being.

Thus, the historical edifice of the Church's social justice work, while weathered by time, stands unshakable, undergirded by a commitment to uphold human dignity in all its forms. This sacred mission calls each generation anew, demanding a response to the cries of the poor and the marginalized. It is in this enduring legacy that the Church finds its strength and its mandate to continue its benevolent work in an ever-changing world.

Indeed, the Church's call to social justice and human dignity is not a relic of the past but a vibrant and urgent mandate for the present and future.

Therein lies the divine charge to uphold, with unwavering resolve, the sacred worth of every human soul.

Case Studies in Social Advocacy within the vast panorama of social justice, the church's role stands as a beacon, illuminating paths toward equity, compassion, and dignity. The sacred institution has not merely advocated in the abstract but has thrown its weight behind tangible causes, manifesting its teachings through concrete actions that reverberate through time and space.

In the first of our studies, we take a sojourn into the heart of Latin America during the tumultuous 20th century. We encounter none other than Archbishop Óscar Romero of El Salvador, a luminary whose life and martyrdom exemplify the Christ-like commitment to justice. Romero, initially perceived as a conservative placater of the ecclesiastical order, underwent a transformation, set aflame by the Holy Spirit and the cries of his impoverished flock. As the scales fell from his eyes, Romero became a vociferous advocate for the marginalized, fearless in speaking truth to power. With a heart brimming with love, he declared, "If God accepts the sacrifice of my life, may my blood be the seed of freedom." Thus, he stood against the machinery of oppression, ultimately laying down his life, a sacrificial lamb in the modern age.

Thence, we move to Africa, where the Apartheid regime wove a fabric of division and disdain, treating human dignity as an ephemeral concept rather than an indelible reality. In this maelstrom, we find Archbishop Desmond Tutu, a towering figure of moral rectitude. Tutu's advocacy was not confined to the pulpit; it permeated the streets, the courtrooms, and the very soul of the South African nation. He invoked the tenets of Ubuntu—a philosophy mirroring Catholic social teaching's emphasis on communal solidarity—to dismantle the walls of segregation. Through his efforts, the Truth and Reconciliation Commission emerged, a platform for healing and restoration, turning swords into ploughshares, thus embodying the spirit of Christ's resurrection and redemption.

The next case ushers us into the squalid tenements of Chicago in the mid-20th century. Here, we are met by the indomitable spirit of Dorothy Day. Co-founder of the Catholic Worker Movement, Day wove the threads of faith and action into a tapestry of radical hospitality. Her Houses of Hospitality served as sanctuaries for the homeless, the hungry, and the hopeless. In Day's worldview, each person who wandered through her doors bore the imago Dei—the image of God—and thus deserved boundless respect and love. Her activism transcended charity, merging with justice as she tirelessly advocated for labor rights, peace, and systemic change. Nay, her Day-by-day (pun intended) actions were not only acts of mercy but also acts of defiance against societal structures that debased the human soul.

Let us traverse the oceans to the shores of India, where Mother Teresa, now Saint Teresa of Calcutta, offers another variegated prism through which we view the Church's unwavering commitment to human dignity. Her work among the "poorest of the poor" in the teeming streets of Calcutta reveals a heart aflame with divine love. Teresa saw not just destitution but the face of Christ in every diseased, destitute individual. Established in 1950, the Missionaries of Charity became the human hands of divine compassion, offering solace and care where society had abandoned any semblance of hope. Her efforts transcended religious boundaries, demonstrating that the Church's mission is universal, grounded in the belief that every human life reflects the inexhaustible glory of the Creator.

This compendium would be incomplete without examining the movements spearheaded by laity, most notably the global reach of the St. Vincent de Paul Society. Founded by Blessed Frédéric Ozanam in the 19th century, this organization exemplifies the lay faithful's power in acting as the Church's hands and feet. Rooted in the Gospel mandate to love thy neighbor, the Society provides not just alms but friendship, acknowledging the inherent dignity in each recipient. Its vocational approach to service—recognizing and responding to the holiness within each individual—stands as a living testament to the Church's teachings on human dignity.

Moreover, a recent exemplar can be discerned in the Church's response to the migrant crisis, particularly in Europe's southern boundaries. Organizations such as Caritas have been relentless in their advocacy for migrants' rights, offering sustenance and sanctuary amidst the storm. Yet, the advocacy transcends immediate relief; it extends to lobbying for humane policies and systemic change, a clarion call to the world to recognize the dignity of those who traverse desolate lands and treacherous seas, seeking solace and safety.

Another significant chapter unfolds in the Middle East, amidst the rubble of conflict and the cries for peace. Here we see the tenacious spirit of Melkite Greek Catholic Archbishop Elias Chacour, champion of non-violence amidst the Israeli-Palestinian conflict. His efforts in establishing educational institutions strive to build bridges of understanding between divided communities. Rooted in the Beatitudes, Chacour's mission dispels the darkness of enmity through the light of education, showcasing the Church's potential as an agent of peace and reconciliation. "We belong to the land of Jesus," he declares, a poignant reminder that peace within the human heart echoes peace within the human community.

Finally, let us not overlook the contributions closer to our epoch, exemplified by the works of Catholic activists in environmental advocacy. Figures like Pope Francis himself offer robust frameworks via encyclicals like "Laudato Si'," marrying scientific insights with theological imperatives. These contributions stress our duty to care for creation, recognizing the intricate links between environmental degradation and social injustice. Grassroots efforts following this theological lead work tirelessly to promote sustainable living, echoing the ancient command to be stewards of God's creation.

These varied case studies reveal a singular truth: the Church, in its advocacy, neither wavers nor wanes. It stands resolute, a bulwark against dehumanization, echoing through its manifold actions the eternal proclamation that every human life is sacred. The Church's engagement in social justice is a mirror, reflecting its deep-seated beliefs about human dignity. One must forever remember and honor that these initiatives, whether rendered through the hands of clergy or laity, embody the very essence of the Church's mission: to uphold and celebrate the inviolable dignity of each and every soul.

And so, from the martyred saints to modern-day activists, the Church's role in social justice—manifested in a plethora of actions and advocacy— is not merely an appendage to its doctrinal corpus but the very heartbeat of its mission. The blood of martyrs, the toil of activists, the prayers of the faithful—all bear witness to a transcendent reality: "Whatsoever you do to the least of my brethren," said our Lord, "you do unto me."

Chapter 8: The Role of Conscience and Moral Decision-Making

In the ceaseless journey through the labyrinthine corridors of moral philosophy, the conscience emerges not as mere accouterment but as the very fulcrum upon which the authenticity of our moral existence pivots. Conscience, in its most hallowed conception, is not simply a construct of the mind but a sanctified voice, an echo of the Divine within us, guiding the soul through the chasms of ethical decision-making. It is through the meticulous cultivation and education of this inner sanctum that one discerns the luminous path of righteousness from the treacherous thickets of moral ambiguity. In this sacred dance, grace intertwines with free will, granting us the fortitude to transcend base inclinations and align our choices with the immutable wisdom of Church teachings. Herein lies the true essence of moral integrity: a symphony of everyday decisions that, in their collective harmony, reflect the sublime order of God's eternal law. Thus, as we navigate the manifold complexities of our temporal existence, the conscientious interplay between divine grace and human freedom becomes the cornerstone of an authentically moral life.

The Nature of Conscience

In the grand theater of human experience, the conscience emerges as an ethereal, internal compass, guiding the soul through the labyrinth of moral quandaries. Hence, conscience is not merely an intellectual faculty but a symphonic harmony of divine whisperings, rational deliberations, and emotive urgencies. Its essence transcends the mere accumulation of human knowledge, reflecting a mystical interplay between divine law and human freedom. As a beacon bestowed by the Eternal, conscience compels us to discern and uphold the good, while eschewing the malevolent. The dignity of the human person is thus inextricably bound to this inner moral tribunal, for it is through a well-formed conscience that one achieves the sublime harmony between faith and action, elevating mundane existence to a plane of divine intentionality and ethical clarity.

Formation and Education of Conscience ...Conscience, that delicate and intricate seed within the mortal breast, requires careful cultivation and vigilant guidance, lest it be marred by neglect or deviation from divine truth. In the heart of every person, it serves as an interior tribunal, discerning right from wrong with an acuity akin to the sharpest blade.

The formation of conscience is paramount, not merely as a singular act but as a lifelong endeavor, demanding both grace and exercise of free will. Much akin to the tender sapling that bends toward the sunlight, so must conscience be subtly and persistently oriented towards the light of divine teachings. It is the sacred duty of both individuals and the Holy Mother Church to foster this growth, ensuring that conscience acts as a faithful arbiter of moral truth.

Firstly, the rudiments of conscience formation lie in early education imbued with the ethos of Christ's teachings. From the youthful days of catechesis, wherein the rudimentary principles are imparted, to the deeper theological reflections in later years, the conscience must be nourished. The bedrock of this moral instruction is Scripture, which imparts the essence of divine law and its application to the myriad dilemmas faced by humanity. Hence, the stories and parables of Holy Writ imbue the pliable mind with the fundamental distinctions between righteousness and iniquity.

Yet, let us not rest upon early instruction alone. The task extends into the vigilant exploration of Tradition and the Magisterium, creating a tapestry of moral wisdom. Conscience, if not continuously enriched, can wither or deviate, like a plant deprived of water. Therefore, engagement with the Holy Sacraments and active participation in the life of the Church are indispensable, providing continuous infusion of grace which aids the conscience in maintaining its true course.

Furthermore, the role of community cannot be understated. It is within the communal bonds of family, parish, and broader ecclesial bodies that one's conscience is tested and refined. These relations provide not only examples to emulate but also forums for moral discourse and reflection.

Just as iron sharpens iron, so does the interchange of moral perspectives within the ecclesia sharpen and fortify the individual conscience.

Additionally, one must be wary of the various modern philosophies and ideologies that besiege the conscience from every direction. A well-formed conscience must learn to discern and sift through the myriad voices clamoring for its allegiance, weighing them against the immutable truths entrusted to the Church by Christ Himself. Such discernment is a refined skill, honed through both study and prayer, illuminated by the light of grace.

Temptations of moral relativism, which pervade our contemporary culture, pose a considerable threat to the formation and education of conscience. The clergy and laity alike must guard against the encroaching belief that all moral truths are subjective or context-dependent. Instead, the teachings of St. Thomas Aquinas remind us of the existence of universal moral laws rooted in the natural order, accessible through right reason and revelation.

Moreover, the Sacrament of Reconciliation plays a pivotal role in the education of conscience. Through the humble admission of sin and the reception of absolution, the penitent's conscience is progressively purified and aligned more precisely with divine law. This sacrament rekindles the latent spark of grace, restoring clarity where confusion has crept in and imparting strength to resist future temptations.

Yet, the task of conscience formation is not solely a matter of avoiding evil but also embracing and effectuating the good. Acts of charity and justice serve to enliven the conscience, furnishing it with a deeper appreciation for the divine command to love one's neighbor as oneself. Through tangible acts of mercy, the abstract principles of moral philosophy are rendered concrete, and the conscience is thereby invigorated.

Lastly, in our pilgrimage toward eternity, the continuous engagement with sacred liturgy and personal prayer cannot be overlooked as pillars in the formation and education of conscience. They are the lifelines that connect the individual soul to the divine source of all moral guidance. The liturgy, with its rich tapestry of symbols, readings, and sacraments, undergirds the conscience in its daily struggles, while personal prayer nurtures an intimate dialogue with the Creator, fostering a disposition of listening and obedience.

In closing, the formation and education of conscience remain an intricate dance between divine grace and human effort, perpetually moving towards the ultimate goal of moral perfection in Christ. Conscientious cultivation, guided by the wisdom of the Church and the illumination of the Holy Spirit, ensures that this inner sanctuary remains pure and true, navigating the tumultuous seas of life with steadfast fidelity to the divine compass.

The Role of Grace and Free Will is so intrinsically woven into the fabric of conscience and moral decision-making that to sever one thread is to unravel an entire moral tapestry. As we dissect the very nature of conscience, we find ourselves inexorably drawn into the interplay between divine grace and human free will, an intricate dance upon which the morality of the Church deeply meditates.

Conscience, that "still small voice" within, guides us toward moral decisions imbued with dignity and righteousness. Yet, this inner moral compass is itself a confluence of two profoundly significant forces: grace and free will. Grace, in its divine generosity and boundlessness, breathes life into the human spirit, imbuing it with a sense of purpose, virtue, and unmerited favor. Free will, on the other hand, gifts the human person with the terrifying and wondrous ability to choose—to walk the path of righteousness or the road to perdition. Together, these entities forge the crucible within which our moral decisions are made.

In the grand scheme of Catholic theology, grace is more than a mere bestowal of divine favor. It is an elevating force that touches the human soul, transforming it, making it capable of acts it could not achieve on its own. St. Augustine of Hippo, in his contemplations, accentuated the importance of this divine aid, viewing grace as an essential component in the moral elevation of the human being. Without grace, the human condition remains crippled under the weight of original sin and the manifold temptations of our fallen nature. Conversely, with grace, the soul can rise above its base instincts, aspiring toward the divine.

Free will, however, stands as the counterpart to grace, providing the individual with the autonomy necessary to act upon that divine gift. St. Thomas Aquinas elucidated that free will is a reflection of God's image in man, emphasizing the dignity bestowed upon the human person as a creature capable of deliberate choice. Through free will, man becomes a moral agent, accountable for his actions, and capable of true virtue. It is within this domain of freedom that the conscience finds its battlefield, where the eternal struggle between good and evil unfolds.

Consider the nature of conscience itself: a divine imprint upon the soul, whispering the truths of moral law, yet vulnerable to the distortions of human desires and external influences. A properly formed conscience, nurtured through grace, aligns itself with the will of God, while the misled conscience, colored by the misuse of free will, strays into moral ambiguity and error. Thus, the role of grace cannot be overstated; it enlightens the conscience, giving clarity to moral truths for the soul that seeks it earnestly.

The Church, recognizing the profound significance of this interplay, emphasizes the role of sacraments as conduits of grace. Through baptism, the initial stain of original sin is washed away, and the soul is infused with sanctifying grace. The Eucharist, the sacrament of love, nourishes the soul, fortifying it with the strength to persist in its moral journey. Confession offers the penitent reconciliation and the restoring grace to mend the ruptures caused by sin. Each sacrament, in its unique manner, administers the grace necessary for the soul's continual moral growth.

As one explores the depths of moral theology, it is evident that grace does not negate free will. Rather, it elevates it, harmonizing human freedom with divine law. Free will, untouched by grace, is likened to a ship adrift without a rudder, subject to the whims of chaotic seas. With grace, that same vessel is given a captain's hand, steering it toward safe harbors of moral certitude. This analogy suffices to demonstrate that human freedom finds its fulfillment not in capricious autonomy but in its alignment with the divine will.

The role of grace and free will in moral decision-making is poignantly illustrated in the lives of the saints, who exemplify the union of human will and divine grace. St. Francis of Assisi, renouncing worldly riches, embraced a life of poverty and humility, driven by the grace that transformed his will. St. Teresa of Avila, through profound prayer and contemplation, surrendered her will to God's, allowing grace to lead her to the heights of spiritual ecstasy and moral rectitude. These luminaries of the faith demonstrate that grace, while necessary, invites human cooperation through the exercise of free will.

Therefore, the nature of conscience is not merely a passive reception of divine truths but an active engagement with them. This engagement is typified by the individual's response to grace and the exercise of free will. A well-formed conscience is the fruit of this synergistic relationship, where grace enlightens and free will chooses to adhere to its guidance. The moral decisions one makes are reflective of this dynamic, evidencing the dignity and worth of the human person as a moral and spiritual agent.

In sum, "The Role of Grace and Free Will" in the context of "The Nature of Conscience" is an exploration of the deepest aspects of our moral existence. It is in understanding and embracing this interplay that one begins to appreciate the profound dignity inherent in the human person. Conscience, when illuminated by grace and exercised through free will, becomes a beacon of moral clarity, guiding one toward a life of virtue and alignment with divine will. The Church, through its teachings and sacraments, continually fosters this relationship, urging the faithful to seek grace and exercise their freedom in accordance with God's moral law. Thus, in the grand design of divine providence, grace and free will are the twin pillars supporting the moral edifice of human dignity.

Practical Application in Moral Choices

In the labyrinth of human existence, the conscience doth serve as an ever-present guide, directing the soul towards choices steeped in virtue. As pilgrims on a shared journey, we are ceaselessly confronted with decisions quotidian and profound, wherein the divine compass of conscience illuminates the path of righteousness. Ever vigilant, the Church offers counsel, rooted in timeless wisdom, to navigate the treacherous waters of moral complexity. Herein is revealed a profound truth: to heed the promptings of a well-formed conscience is to embrace the dignity bestowed upon each person by the Creator, upholding moral integrity even as the shadows of modernity encroach. Thus, in the dance of daily life and its multifaceted dilemmas, the conscience stands as the silent sentinel, urging fidelity to the celestial order and safeguarding the sanctity of human choice.

Everyday Decisions and Moral Integrity are the primordial theatres wherein our conscience performs. Day by day, in the minutiae that define our mortal tenure, the crucible of moral integrity is forged most steadfastly. In those seemingly inconsequential moments—the ephemeral pauses between breaths, the silent decisions made when none are there to witness—the conscience speaks, directing the soul toward virtue or vice.

It is in the mundane and the routine that the true essence of moral fiber is often displayed. Consider the myriad choices one encounters daily: the decision to speak truth or remain silent, the determination to show kindness or indifference, to act justly or selfishly. These decisions, woven into the fabric of our existence, delineate the contours of our moral landscape. A survey of common interactions reveals much. Is one honest in dealings, considerate toward the neighbor, mindful of the other's dignity? Such inquiries are not mere moral exercises but questions upon which hinges eternal welfare.

For instance, the choice to lend a helping hand to a colleague in distress, though minor in the grand scheme, resonates with profound ethical ramifications. Beneath the surface of that simple act lies the bedrock of Christian charity and respect for human dignity. One's moral integrity is subtly validated by such acts, and they accrue over time, painting a portrait of conscience-responsive life.

When navigating the labyrinth of quotidian life, moral integrity anchors the vessel of the soul amidst the tempest of temptations and ethical dilemmas. Each decision, no matter how apparently trivial, forms a brushstroke in the larger tapestry of one's character. Herein lies the genius of Divine Providence, that even the smallest deed contributes to the edifice of virtue or vice.

Moreover, moral integrity takes a manifold form when cast against the backdrop of modernity. Consider financial honesty in everyday practice— such as reporting accurate figures on a tax form or not pilfering supplies from one's workplace. The conscience, illuminated by divine grace, discerns right from wrong, even when secular society tends toward moral relativism. It is this unwavering adherence to righteousness in daily transactions that delineates the Christian moral agent from the ethically indifferent.

Yet, while the call to uphold moral integrity in daily decisions is clear, it is not without its challenges. Human frailty, enticements of the flesh, societal pressures—each conspires to cloud judgment and complicate moral choices. Here, the Church's teachings serve as a lighthouse, guiding the faithful through ethical ambiguity. Catechism provides structured reflection, assisting the believer in understanding how Christ's commandments apply to even the most minor of daily actions.

Not to be overlooked is the formative power of community. Through the living witness of others, one sees the abstract principles of moral integrity embodied. When members of the faithful act with consistent righteousness in their everyday dealings, they offer a silent yet potent testimony to the efficacy of living a conscience-driven life. Whether it be a parent modeling honesty to children or friends supporting each other against moral compromise, communal integrity reinforces individual resolve.

The Sermon on the Mount, perhaps one of the most eloquent articulations of Christian ethics, is equally applicable to the moments of day-to-day life as it is to grand moral struggles. "Let your light so shine before men, that they may see your good works, and glorify your Father which is in heaven" (Matthew 5:16). This illumination does not merely refer to extraordinary acts of valor or sanctity but extends to every small gesture performed in alignment with divine will.

Engaging in societal interactions inevitably poses ethical questions requiring discernment. Whether pondering fair trade practices when making consumer decisions or considering the equitable distribution of one's resources, moral integrity directs these choices. The individual must constantly return to the inner sanctum of their conscience, seeking divine wisdom in the allocation of their material and spiritual resources.

Furthermore, daily decisions often require balancing multiple moral goods—a truly Shakespearean dilemma. One might face the choice of investing time in family or in community service, each a virtuous commitment but demanding sacrifice. Here, moral integrity does not dictate a singular path but invites prudential judgment, seasoned by prayer and reflection.

Lastly, consider how self-sacrifice and moderation in personal habits bear witness to moral integrity. In a culture besieged by hedonism and excess, the tempered choices of a moderate life mark a profound moral stance. Decisions about consumption, leisure, and relations are thus transformed into acts of defiance against moral turpitude, aligning one's life more closely with Christian virtues.

It is through these myriad, humble choices that moral integrity is both tested and proven. A soul attuned to God's grace will invariably find itself making decisions that echo with righteousness, navigating the complexities of life with an inner compass steadfastly pointing toward heavenly virtue and dignity. The aggregate of such choices becomes a testament not only to personal character but also to the transformative power of conscience guided by divine will.

Complex Issues and Church Guidance seamlessly intertwines with "The Role of Conscience and Moral Decision-Making," specifically in the section "Practical Application in Moral Choices." In this mosaic of the human spirit, the conscience stands as both sentinel and spearhead, navigating the labyrinthine corridors of ethics. As we traverse this terrain, the guidance of Holy Mother Church becomes paramount, for in complex issues, the light of ecclesiastical wisdom is indispensable.

Not all moral questions yield easily to the individual's internal compass. In these moments, the Church acts as a lighthouse amid the stormy seas of ethical perplexity. When dilemmas such as euthanasia or reproductive technologies arise, the conscience may find itself ensnared in the thicket of modern relativism. Here, the Church offers not merely doctrinal pronouncements but a compassionate embrace guiding the faithful toward Truth. The Magisterium, through its teachings, illuminates these challenging pathways with the clarity of Divine Revelation.

St. Thomas Aquinas reminds us that conscience is the voice of God echoing within the human heart, yet it does not function in a vacuum. It requires nurturing and enlightenment through prayer, Scripture, and the Sacraments. Particularly in intricate moral issues, the Church's role extends beyond a didactic one; it is pastoral, aiding individuals to form their consciences genuinely and robustly. The faithful are called to engage with the Church's teachings actively, thereby transforming complex issues into opportunities for spiritual growth.

Consider bioethical quandaries, which are fraught with scientific advancements and moral hazards. The Church, through documents like *Humanae Vitae* and *Evangelium Vitae*, provides a moral framework that respects the sanctity of life and human dignity. The discrete guidance from these teachings allows the faithful to navigate the perils of modern bioethics with an informed conscience. The wisdom imparted by the Church serves as a bulwark against the ethical erosion perpetuated by contemporary secularism.

Moreover, socio-economic dilemmas solicit the Church's voice of guidance. Catholic Social Teaching, with its principles of Subsidiarity and

Solidarity, acts as a compass for the faithful in navigating issues such as economic disparity and social injustice. The conscientiously formed individual, guided by these teachings, becomes an agent of transformation in the world. Here again, the Church's guidance transfigures complex socio-economic issues into canvases for moral action and social righteousness.

The role of grace in moral decision-making must not be understated. As St. Augustine posited, grace is not merely the soul's adornment but its very life-force. The Church, through its sacraments, dispenses this grace, enabling the conscience to soar above the morass of moral ambiguities. It is within the sacramental life that one finds the strength to confront ethical complexities with courage and fidelity to Divine Will. The Confessional, in particular, is a font of grace, restoring the soul's equilibrium and enlightening the conscience.

In more personal moral quandaries, such as relational ethics or career decisions, the Church's pastoral guidance remains vital. The vocation of marriage, for instance, is not merely a romantic ideal but a covenantal reality imbued with moral responsibility. The Church's teachings on matrimonial ethics provide clear, divine directives for marital fidelity, thereby safeguarding the sanctity of this sacred bond amid societal attempts to redefine it. Similarly, in the realm of professional ethics, the Church's doctrine on the dignity of labor guides the faithful in making morally sound career decisions that reflect the inherent value of the human person.

The Church's guidance also permeates the intricate realm of political engagement. When faced with legislative choices that bear moral implications, a well-formed conscience turns to the principles of Natural Law and the social teachings of the Church. Documents such as *Gaudium et Spes* and *Caritas in Veritate* elucidate the moral dimensions of socio-political involvement. They counsel the faithful to act not out of partisan fervor but from a commitment to justice, peace, and the common good. Thus, political decisions, often fraught with complexity, become opportunities for witnessing to the Gospel's transformative power.

The mosaic of modern moral challenges often includes environmental ethics, where the stewardship of God's creation is in peril. The Church's encyclical *Laudato Si'* brings forth an integrated approach to environmental and human ecology, urging the conscience to consider the broader implications of ecological negligence. By embracing the Church's guidance, the faithful can transform environmental stewardship from a complex issue into a testament of reverence for God's creation, driven by a conscientious commitment to sustainability and justice for future generations.

Lastly, the profound implications of advancing technologies in artificial intelligence and robotics introduce fresh moral conundrums. The Church, through its enduring wisdom, addresses these issues with the principles of human dignity and the common good. As stated in numerous Vatican documents and conference declarations, technological innovation must serve humanity, not the other way around. Guided by these teachings, the conscience can navigate the ethical intricacies of the digital age, ensuring that technological advancements align with the moral imperatives of justice and human dignity.

In these manifold arenas of moral complexity, the Church's guidance serves as a steadfast beacon, illuminating the path for the Christian disciple. Conscience, while deeply personal, is never isolated; it is formed, informed, and transformed within the nourishing bosom of the Church's tradition and teachings. The faithful, heeding this divine pedagogy, find the strength to confront and resolve ethical quandaries with moral integrity and unwavering faith.

To conclude, the harmonious interplay between the Church's guidance and the individual's conscience in the face of complex moral issues underscores the divine architecture of moral decision-making. It is through this sacred synergy that the faithful are equipped to illuminate the world with the light of Christ, transforming the complexities of moral life into a sublime symphony of divine love and human dignity.

Chapter 9: Human Rights and Catholic Teaching

Verily, in the grand tapestry of human existence, the Church doth stand as a vigilant sentinel, guarding the sanctity of rights bestowed upon each soul by the Divine Creator. The Church's stance on human rights, forged through sacred documents and hallowed decrees, maintains an unwavering reverence for the innate dignity of humankind. Rooted in the Gospel and enriched by centuries of theological discourse, these teachings affirm that every individual, fashioned in the image of the Almighty, merits respect and justice irrespective of age, status, or condition. Manifest in modern pronouncements, the Church endeavours mightily to align temporal rights with eternal truths, resolving conflicts through a prism of moral clarity. Thus, the arduous path toward harmonizing secular edicts with sacrosanct principles is trod, fraught with practical challenges, yet illuminated by the light of divine wisdom.

The Church's Stance on Human Rights

The Church, ever unwavering in her impassioned defense of the sacred worth of humanity, posits that the very essence of human rights lies not in mere social constructs but in the divinely bestowed dignity of each soul. Rooted in the Church's rich theological heritage and the timeless teachings of Holy Scripture, the Church avows that human rights are inextricably linked to the Imago Dei, the divine image bestown upon all by the Creator. This unwavering stance manifests in the Church's robust affirmations and solemn declarations, underscoring the sanctity of life from conception to natural death, the inviolable liberty of conscience, and the intrinsic worth of every person, regardless of station or circumstance. In the face of modern societal upheavals and moral relativism, this stance remains a steadfast beacon, guiding the faithful to uphold justice, mercy, and love, alike.

Core Documents and Declarations form the bedrock upon which the Church's stance on human rights is immovably founded. A beacon of sacred texts and solemn pronouncements, these documents not only articulate the Church's profound respect for human dignity but also assert the moral teachings that enshrine the inviolable nature of the human person.

Preeminent among these cornerstone texts is the *Universal Declaration of Human Rights*, an instrument of paramount import endorsed by the Holy See. Though not of ecclesiastical origin, this declaration echoes the Church's own conviction in the universal and inalienable rights bestowed upon every individual by their Creator. It is a confluence where secular propositions dovetail with divine truths, forming a harmonious melody that extols the sanctity of human life and its inherent rights.

The magisterial voice of the Church also reverberates through the encyclicals, those epistolary treasures calqued with both grandeur and gravity. Particularly noteworthy is *Pope John XXIII's Pacem in Terris*, which delineates a comprehensive vision for peace rooted in the respect for human rights. Declaring unequivocally that every human being is a person endowed with intelligence and free will, this encyclical renders a clarion call to uphold these intrinsic rights, laying a moral groundwork for civil and ecclesiastical society alike.

Gaudium et Spes, a pastoral constitution from the Second Vatican Council, adds a vibrant color to the rich tapestry of the Church's teachings on human dignity. Emblematically proclaiming that 'whatever is opposed to life itself... whatever insults human dignity...' should be 'infamy.' This document stands as a testament to the Church's unwavering commitment to advocate for human rights even amid the vexing complexities of the modern age.

Moreover, the robust pronouncements in *Evangelium Vitae* by *Pope John Paul II* cast a luminous spotlight on the paramount value of life. This encyclical ascends to the theological summits in denouncing the contemporary 'culture of death' and advocating for a 'culture of life.' By doing so, it reinforces the Church's commitment to protecting the fundamental rights of every human being, from conception to natural death.

The manifold teachings of the Church have not been confined to abstruse theologians nor relegated to dusty tomes. They manifest in declarations like *Pope Paul VI's Populorum Progressio,* wherein the development and well-being of all peoples is exalted as a prime concern of peace. This encyclical envisions a world where human rights are not only acknowledged but also actively pursued, ensuring that the divine principle of justice transcends all human endeavors.

Furthermore, it would be remiss to overlook the substantial contribution of *Dignitatis Humanae,* the Declaration on Religious Freedom issued by the Second Vatican Council. This document profoundly affirms that religious liberty emanates from the very dignity of the human person. It posits that no one should be coerced into acting contrary to their conscience, thus underscoring a pivotal aspect of human rights—even as it enjoins respect for truth and moral order.

While ecclesial doctrines have been historically filtered through Latin theological lenses, the Church's recent addressal of human rights issues employs an accessible and universal discourse. The *Compendium of the Social Doctrine of the Church,* a modern magnum opus, succinctly encapsulates the Church's teachings on social issues, grounding its discourse in the primacy of human dignity and the common good. It serves as a vital resource for grasping the connective tissue binding human rights and Catholic social teaching.

Pastoral letters and apostolic exhortations likewise continue to breathe life into the Church's human rights dialogue. *Pope Francis's Evangelii Gaudium* (The Joy of the Gospel) critiques the idolatry of money and advocates for economic justice, thereby resonating with the perennial plea for the respect and protection of human rights. In the same vein, *Laudato Si'* (On Care for Our Common Home) intertwines ecological concerns with human dignity, challenging the faithful to view the care for creation as an extension of their commitment to human rights.

A veritable font of wisdom and counsel, these core documents and declarations delineate a vision that deeply intertwines the sacred with the secular. They stand as stalwart witnesses to the Church's enduring advocacy for human dignity, imperatively calling upon all adherents of faith to engage actively in the realization of these noble principles. Hence, while the temporal realm grapples with the evolving lexicon of human rights, the eternal truths articulated through the Church's magisterial teachings provide the immutable moral compass guiding believers toward a just and dignified existence for all.

Human Rights in Modern Church Teaching finds its place within the broader context of *The Church's Stance on Human Rights*, projecting a radiant path through the realms of modernity and sacred tradition. In our tumultuous age, rife with manifold calls for justice and cries for dignity, one must ponder upon how the ancient yet timeless teachings of the Church resound through the corridors of contemporary civilization.

The annals of history whisper with the steadfast voices of ecclesiastical luminaries, who, through successive epochs, had intonated the inviolable dignity of each human soul. Yet, it is in the papal documents since Vatican II that we perceive the Church's elucidation on human rights most crystalline. Amidst an evolving societal landscape, the Church, attuned to the zeitgeist, speaks with renewed vigor in defense of the oppressed and marginalized.

Consider, for instance, the seminal encyclical *Pacem in Terris* (1963) by Pope John XXIII, which presents not merely an echo but a resounding affirmation of universal human rights. It delineates these rights not as abstractions but as concrete entitlements that arise from the dignity inherent in every human being. These include the rights to life, bodily integrity, and the necessities requisite for human decency, such as food, shelter, and a just wage.

Herein, the Church's position diverges notably from secular humanism, which sometimes veers into the quicksands of relativism. The Holy See, while recognizing the shared aspirations towards human rights, anchors these rights in a higher, divine ordinance. Rights, the Church posits, are not merely granted by human institutions but are inscribed in the very nature of the human person by the Creator.

Aye, this theological foundation imparts a profound sanctity to human rights, setting them apart from mere legislative constructs. In documents like *Gaudium et Spes* (1965), the Church expounds on humanity's social nature and responsibilities. It asserts that true social progress cannot be achieved without acknowledging the moral and spiritual imperatives that underpin human dignity.

Moreover, modern encyclicals such as *Centesimus Annus* (1991), by Pope John Paul II, revisit and ponder anew upon the social doctrines of the Church in the light of contemporary challenges. Capitalism and socialism, democracy and totalitarianism—these worldly systems are weighed not by their temporal successes but by their adherence to and promotion of authentic human development.

The encyclical *Evangelium Vitae* (1995), also by Pope John Paul II, inveighs against the "culture of death" prevalent in modern societies. In stark contrast, it proclaims a "culture of life" wherein every human being, from conception to natural death, is valued and protected. This dynamic polarity reflects an unwavering commitment to the sanctity of life, an aspect intrinsically linked to human rights.

Furthermore, Pope Francis, in his encyclical *Fratelli Tutti* (2020), calls for a global fraternity that transcends borders and cultural divisions. He laments the throwaway culture and the myriad injustices that plague our world, urging a collective recognition of the inherent dignity of all people. His words underscore the imperative of caring for the poor, the refugee, the stranger—which serves as a testament to the enduring relevance of Catholic teaching on human rights.

These encyclicals, together with various Vatican documents, do not merely articulate principles—they bind the faithful to a social mission. They direct us towards active engagement in public life, urging Christians to be the leaven within society, promoting justice and peace.

Therefore, in juxtaposing the Church's timeless teachings with the evolving discourse on human rights, one discovers an enduring truth. Not of this world, yet profoundly involved in it, the Church heralds a vision of human rights that transcends mere legality and champions the sacred dignity of every individual. With unwavering resolve, it beckons the faithful to echo its clarion call in every arena of human endeavor.

Aligning Secular and Sacred Rights

In the grand tapestry of human existence, a delicate balance must be struck between the rights proclaimed by secular institutions and the sacred truths upheld by the Church. The harmonious alignment of these rights is essential for the genuine realization of human dignity in its fullest form. Recognizing this, one must delve into the intricate dance where secular principles frequently find a reflective echo in the moral teachings of Catholicism. While secular rights oft champion liberty and equality, the Church propounds a divine origin of human worth, grounding these concepts in the imago Dei—the belief that man is created in the image of God. This crossroad evokes a synthesis where laws of the state, when infused with moral compassions articulated by the Church, can craft a civilization that honors both temporal justice and eternal truths. It is within this confluence that moral theologians, Roman Catholics, and sociologists alike must navigate, striving to reconcile the temporary with the eternal, and the human with the divine.

Conflicts and Resolutions have ever embroiled the relationship between secular human rights and the sacred tenets taught by the Church, both striving to affirm the innate dignity of the human person. This alignment, fraught with friction and dissonances, forms one of the crucial undertakings of our apologetical endeavor, seeking to bridge chasms that divide the secular from the sacred. While both realms affirm the value inherent in human life, their divergent approaches and foundational premises sometimes lead to discord.

In the secular domain, the conception of human rights often rests upon principles of individual autonomy and freedom, a legacy of the Enlightenment. This framework posits that each individual, by virtue of sheer humanity, possesses a set of inalienable rights. Not so different, the sacred teachings of the Church assert the sanctity of human life, shaped by divine image and grace, thus endowing each person with profound dignity. The crux of the conflict lies in the grounding of these rights; secular thought seeks rationality devoid of transcendence, while sacred teaching imbues rights with divine import.

One prominent flashpoint in this dialectic is the question of bioethics—particularly in matters of abortion and euthanasia. Secular human rights argue for the sovereignty of personal choice and bodily autonomy, often advocating for the permissibility of such acts under a regime of individual rights. Conversely, Catholic teaching staunchly upholds the sanctity of life from conception to natural death, interpreting these acts as violations of divine law and human dignity. Here, the resolution must navigate a delicate path, harmonizing respect for individual autonomy with an unwavering commitment to the sanctity of life as sacrosanct.

Another realm of contention arises in the understanding of social justice. Secular frameworks frequently emphasize equality, non-discrimination, and the material well-being of individuals. The Church, through its social teachings, advocates for a preferential option for the poor, solidarity among peoples, and a vision of the common good that transcends mere material provision. While both aims are noble, their methodologies and ultimate visions may conflict. Resolution, then, requires a synthesis that embraces the material and spiritual dimensions of justice, fostering both temporal welfare and eternal beatitude.

The principle of subsidiarity offers fertile ground for reconciliation. This Catholic social teaching asserts that matters ought to be handled by the smallest, most local competent authority, yet with higher orders ready to assist when necessary. It resonates with secular proponents of decentralization and local governance, although their motivations may differ. By embracing subsidiarity, both secular and sacred paradigms can find common ground, ensuring that the dignity and rights of individuals are best preserved through close-to-home decision-making while retaining a framework for overarching support.

Human sexual ethics presents yet another battleground, particularly in the domains of marriage and family life. Secular rights movements often advocate for the redefinition of marriage and family structures to encompass a broad spectrum of relationships. Catholic teaching, however, adheres to a sacramental view of marriage as a union between one man and one woman, ordered towards procreation and mutual self-giving. Resolving these conflicts requires a return to first principles and a re-examination of the ends and purposes of human sexuality, undergirded by a profound respect for personal dignity and calls for authentic relationships.

The reconciliation between secular and sacred perspectives is not merely an intellectual exercise but requires profound pastoral sensitivity and engagement. The Church must endeavor to understand and empathize with the lived experiences of individuals who navigate secular frameworks while presenting its teachings as paths to true freedom and fulfillment. Through dialogue, education, and witness, the sacred teachings can illuminate the aspirations of secular rights, offering deeper meanings and ultimate fulfillment without compromising core doctrinal positions.

Indeed, the role of conscience emerges prominently in these conflicts and their resolutions. The Church teaches that a well-formed conscience, aligned with divine law, guides moral and ethical decisions. In contrast, secular viewpoints often champion the primacy of individual conscience, albeit sometimes without the anchor of a moral absolute. Herein lies an avenue for resolution through the education and formation of conscience, harmonizing personal autonomy with moral responsibility and divine truth. A properly formed conscience can bridge the gap between secular self-determination and sacred obedience to divine will.

Engaging with secular authorities and institutions also bears potential for significant resolution. Through engagement, dialogue, and cooperative ventures, the Church can witness to the Gospel's transformative power, advocating for human rights consistent with divine law. Collaborative initiatives in areas such as healthcare, education, and social services can serve as platforms where secular and sacred values converge for the common good. By working together towards shared goals, both realms can cultivate an environment that honors the dignity of every person.

Resolving conflicts necessitates a prophetic voice that fearlessly upholds the truth while practicing profound charity. The Church is called to be a light in a world that at times, finds itself in moral twilight. This entails unwavering adherence to its teachings on human dignity, the sanctity of life, and the common good, even while engaging in dialogue with secular advocates. True resolution is not mere compromise but a bold, loving proclamation of the full truth about the human person as revealed by God.

It is thus that practical challenges and solutions must be approached with both patience and urgency. In educational systems, the Church should advocate for curricula that offer a holistic view of human dignity, integrating both secular and sacred perspectives. In the public square, Catholics are called to be both citizens and evangelists, advocating for policies and practices that reflect the full dignity of the human person. Through robust catechesis, ongoing formation, and active witness, Catholics can navigate these conflicts, offering resolutions that respect both the rights and the deeper sacred worth of every person.

Ultimately, the endeavor of aligning secular and sacred rights is not an endpoint but a journey. Each generation faces its own set of challenges and conflicts, requiring fresh applications of immutable principles. By steadfastly upholding the dignity given by God, engaging in sincere dialogue, and working towards the common good, Catholics can contribute to a world where the sacred and secular are not adversaries but partners in the noble enterprise of human flourishing.

Practical Challenges and Solutions In the realm where the sacred and the secular intersect, there exists a panorama of complexities that cast shadows over the harmonious alignment of human rights and Catholic teaching. The disparities betwixt the immovable divine decrees and the fluid, ever-evolving nature of secular legislation provide a fertile ground for discord and controversy. How then may the Church navigate these turbulent waters, to claim both fidelity to its sacred tenets and responsiveness to the exigencies of modernity?

Thus, we begin by considering the perennial friction between the indelibility of human rights and the mutable dispositions of secular governance. One might argue that the cornerstone of Catholic teaching on human rights is the inherent dignity of the human person, derived from being imago Dei, made in the image of God. However, when the axioms of human sanctity clash with secular policies—be they concerning life, family, or freedom of expression—the Church is tasked with a delicate balancing act.

One notable paradigm of such clash concerns the sanctity of life vis-à-vis the secular endorsement of practices like abortion and euthanasia. The Catholic Church remains firm on its pro-life stance, viewing all life from conception to natural death as sacred and inviolable. Yet, secular laws in numerous jurisdictions offer differing perspectives, often prioritizing personal autonomy and rights over the unborn or the terminally ill. How, then, can the Church advocate for its unwavering principles in a pluralistic society?

The first pragmatic approach is through robust advocacy and education. The Church ought to engage in the public square, wielding its rich tradition of reasoned argumentation to enlighten and persuade. Efforts may manifest in scholarly articles, public lectures, and active participation in legislative processes. Through these means, the Church can elucidate the philosophical and theological foundations underpinning its teachings on human dignity, thereby casting light upon the moral implications of secular legislation.

But in the ecclesial commitment to upholding sacred rights, mere rhetoric is inadequately equipped to surmount the vast secular edifices of contemporary socio-political landscapes. This brings us to a vital stratagem: collaboration. By forming alliances with like-minded organizations, both religious and secular, the Church can strengthen its voice. Such coalitions may include human rights groups, pro-life organizations, and other entities that share common moral ground.

In addition, the role of lay Catholics cannot be overstated. Empowering the laity to live out and advocate for the Church's teachings in their daily lives, workplaces, and political arenas establishes a grassroots movement that complements hierarchical efforts. Lay Catholics, through their witness and participation in civic affairs, can become agents of transformation, permeating society with the Gospel values of life and dignity.

Another formidable challenge lies in the domain of marriage and family. Herein lies a juxtaposition of sacred belief in the sanctity of matrimony, as a divine covenant between man and woman, against secular inclinations towards redefining marriage and family structures. The Church insists upon the sacramental nature of marriage and its role in the procreation and education of children. However, dissenting secular agendas promote varied familial configurations and individual lifestyle choices as human rights.

Solutions to such dissonance might encompass pastoral initiatives focused on strengthening Catholic families. Pre-marital and matrimonial catechesis can edify couples on the theological richness and societal benefits of traditional marriage. Support systems for families, discussions on faithful parenting, and the celebration of family life can reinforce the Church's teachings in practical and relatable contexts.

While the Church must hold steadfastly to its sacramental understanding of marriage, it also must extend pastoral charity to individuals who live in differing familial situations. Not as an act of concession, but as an expression of Christ's love and a call to deeper conversion. Pastoral outreach programs can be designed to welcome all while clearly delineating the fullness of the Church's doctrine.

Similarly, the question of religious freedom posits a labyrinthine challenge in aligning sacred rights with secular principles. The Church has long upheld that every person has a fundamental right to religious freedom, underpinned by the innate dignity of conscience. However, in various parts of the world, this freedom is curtailed or manipulated to subordinate religious practice to state edicts.

Addressing these challenges involves both local and global advocacy. At the local level, Catholics are called to be vigilant in defending their right to religious expression, whether through legal challenges, public awareness campaigns, or peaceful protest. Globally, the Church must work alongside international bodies to champion the cause of religious freedom, highlighting instances of persecution and lobbying for protection under international law.

The practical considerations also touch upon issues of social justice and moral responsibility. The Church's mission to uphold the dignity of every person entails an unwavering commitment to social justice. Yet, the pursuit of justice often encounters impediments in the form of unjust laws, systemic inequality, and cultural opposition. The Church's preferential option for the poor mandates action, yet secular mechanisms to alleviate poverty sometimes diverge from Catholic ethical principles.

Here, the Church's solution lies in manifest acts of charity and justicemaking. Through its social doctrines, material aid, and advocacy for equitable policies, the Church can bridge the gap between moral teachings and social realities. Catholic social services, just business practices, and community engagement serve as witnesses to the Church's holistic vision of human dignity.

In conclusion, aligning secular and sacred rights presents numerous practical challenges, yet the tapestry of solutions woven with advocacy, education, collaboration, pastoral care, and active engagement in societal processes offers a hopeful path forward. The Church, rooted in the timeless truths of the Gospel, must navigate the ever-changing tides of secular legislation with unwavering fidelity and informed pragmatism. Through this intricate dance, the sanctity of human dignity can be more fully realized in our contemporary epoch.

Chapter 10: The Interplay Between Science and Human Dignity

Amidst the ceaseless march of scientific progress, we find ourselves at a crossroads where the sanctity of human dignity and the promise of technological advancement confront each other. Science in its unbridled pursuit lays bare secrets hitherto enshrouded in divine mystery, yet it is within this unveiling that the Church stands firm, asserting the sacred worth of the human person. Advances in fields such as medical science and genetic engineering challenge us to balance faith and reason, calling for ethical guidelines that preserve human dignity in the face of such profound change. The Church's teachings illuminate a path where the marvels of scientific discovery harmonize with the moral imperatives bestowed by divine wisdom. Thus, it is not the cold calculus of innovation that shall guide us but the enduring principles of our faith, ensuring that every human, from the unborn to the elderly, is treated with the reverence due to beings created in the image of God.

Scientific Discoveries and Church Response

In an age where the tapestry of human understanding ever unfolds, the tides of scientific discovery hath presented both marvels and quandaries to the sacred corridors of the Church. Wherefore, as the revelations of the natural world waxed potent with the advent of new knowledge, the Church, divinely inspired, hath not retreated into obfuscation. Nay, it hath endeavored to align the celestial truths with terrestrial insights, holding steadfast to the premise that each human soul, crafted in the imago Dei, bears indelible value. Thus, the Church doth scrutinize the advancements in realms such as medical science and genetic engineering with a discerning eye, measuring each against the immutable canon of human dignity. It hath responded not with parochial fear but with robust theological discourse, fostering a milieu wherein faith and reason embrace, undergirded by an ethical framework that seeks the elevation of every human spirit. This synthesis of divine doctrine and empirical inquiry ensures that the march of progress doth not tread upon the sanctity of the human person, but rather, exalts it to the glory of the Creator.

Advances in Medical Science witness to the ceaseless endeavor of human ingenuity—beholden not merely to the pursuit of knowledge but ultimately to the sacred guarding of human dignity. In an epoch marked by iconic strides within the realms of medical intervention, diagnostic precision, and therapeutic innovation, we encounter the sublime and daunting intersection of science and moral theology. The Church, in Her wisdom and perennial commitment to the sanctity of life, enters this dialogue with a voice both ancient and ever anew, articulating a balance between the promise of medical advancements and the immutable dignity of the human person.

The marvels of modern medicine, from intricate surgical techniques to revolutionary pharmacological discoveries, indeed present humanity with the gift of extended life and the amelioration of suffering. This has engendered a milieu wherein infirmities once deemed terminal now find remedy, and chronic afflictions meet their palliatives. Such advances, however, bring forth an imperative: the necessity to align these medical miracles with principles that honor the full dignity of the human soul. The Church, rooted in the moral compass of Her teachings, strives to harmonize the scientific with the sacred, guiding the faithful through the labyrinth of ethical quandaries.

In viewing the panorama of medical marvels, one must reflect on the Church's position on practices such as organ transplantation. The seamless act of bestowing life through the gift of an organ, when conducted within ethically delineated frameworks, resonates with the tenets of charity and self-sacrifice. Yet, herein lies the fertility of ethical dilemmas: the procurement of organs must adhere to the inviolable respect of the donor's autonomy and life. It behooves the moral theologian to ponder not merely the technical success of transplantation but its consonance with an unwavering respect for human personhood.

Vaccination, in its enigma of offering immunity against scourges, equally prompts dialogue that melds scientific triumph with ecclesiastical prudence. The eradication of diseases through vaccines heralds an epoch of collective well-being, safeguarded by herd immunity. Nonetheless, the origin and development of certain vaccines, particularly those echoed by the use of embryonic cell lines, demand a rigorous ethical inspection. The Church, while advocating for the common good and public health, propounds that the moral rectitude of these medical interventions must not transgress the sanctity of nascent life.

Stem cell research similarly invites profound theological discourse. Embodying the quintessence of therapeutic promise, stem cells unlock potential in regenerative medicine and the treatment of formidable maladies. Yet, the moral landscape is fraught with the disquieting use of embryonic stem cells, wherein the destruction of embryonic life stirs contention with the Church's pro-life doctrine. The exploration of alternative sources, such as adult stem cells, emerges as a scientifically and ethically harmonious path, reflecting a synthesis wherein medical progress and sacred dignity coexist.

Thus, in the realm of medical genetics, the clinical application of technologies such as CRISPR holds the peril and promise of altering the very blueprint of life. Genetic editing, with its capacity to eliminate congenital maladies, offers new hope yet simultaneously treads perilously toward eugenic practices. The Church's stance, founded on the inherent worth of every human being, contends that genetic manipulation must be constrained by the natural law, preserving the genetic integrity gifted by the Creator.

The quandaries of end-of-life care, resplendent with ethical intricacies, embody an area where medical science and Church teachings converge palpably. Palliative care, enacted with compassion and devoid of the intention to hasten death, epitomizes an avenue where human dignity is paramount. The deliberate withholding or withdrawal of futile medical interventions, when attuned to patient autonomy and comfort, aligns with the Church's moral framework, advocating for a death that honors life's sanctity even in its twilight.

Moreover, the advent of artificial intelligence in diagnostics and patient care introduces both optimism and caution. The promise of precision medicine, and the efficacy of AI in predicting and preventing disease, offers palpable advancements. Yet, this domain calls for stringent moral oversight to ensure that algorithms do not depersonalize patient care, reducing individuals to mere data points, but maintain the inherent dignity afforded to each person as made in the image of God.

The incessant progression of medical science beckons a perennial dialogue with the ecclesiastical authority, a dialogue that seeks not the quenching of innovation but its ethical illumination—a convergence of faith and reason. The Church, while embracing the therapeutic promise of medical advancements, consistently interrogates the moral implication of each new frontier, ensuring that technological prowess never eclipses the divine worth of the human person. Hence, this interplay entrusts to the moral theologian a discerning heart and a vigilant spirit, ever engaged in the noble endeavor of safeguarding human dignity amidst the tides of scientific progress.

In conclusion, the symbiotic relationship between advances in medical science and the Church's ethical teachings serves as a beacon, guiding humanity through the complexities of innovation with a steadfast commitment to the sanctity and dignity of life. It is a relationship that mandates perpetual vigilance, rooted in an unwavering belief in the sacred worth of each human soul, irrespective of the marvels or challenges that medical progress may present. Thus, the faithful are called to approach each new medical discovery not merely with hope but with a conscientious reverence for the divine image reflected in every person.

Genetic Engineering and Human Ethics and as we delve into the intersection of scientific advancement and the eternal verities cherished by the Church, we stand at a crossroads where miracles of modernity greet the perennial truths of human dignity. Genetic engineering, a tome of uncharted potential and peril, demands our scrutiny and sagacity. The heralds of such remarkable discoveries—though heralding from the bastion of scientific endeavor—must be balanced against the sanctified ethos that guards human worth.

Verily, the realm of genetic engineering unleashes both marvel and menace. To splice the helix of life, to tamper with the blueprint of our existence, is to grasp the very essence of Creation. But what doth it profit a man if he gain the power to alter his being but forsake his soul's sanctity? One must tread cautiously, for the endeavors to engineer the human genome conjure images of a modern Babel, where humanity's hubris seeks to usurp divine prerogatives.

From the era of the Apostles, the Church has maintained an unwavering beacon of ethical guidance amidst the shifting sands of human achievement. Yet, in the face of genetic engineering, her response is rooted not in fear of progress but in the defense of immutable dignity. This is the very essence of the Church's doctrinal posture, as revealed through councils and catechism, over epochs.

Theological luminaries have long pondered the nature of man's dominion over creation. Saint Augustine's ruminations on human nature and Aquinas's expositions on the sacred personage both resonate through this discourse. Genetic engineering, thus, compels us to revisit these foundational teachings, as we balance innovation with reverence. Shall we, like Prometheus, steal fire from the gods and thus condemn ourselves to perpetual torment?

The confluence of ecclesial teaching and scientific discovery is not inherently antagonistic. Indeed, the Church acknowledges the boon of medical advances, applauding when such knowledge alleviates suffering and extends life within the bounds of moral consideration. However, the engineering of human life itself transcends mere scientific progression; it touches upon the very sanctity of God's design.

It behooves us to question the ethical ramifications of altering genetic makeup to eradicate disease or enhance human traits. The specter of eugenics looms large, a grim reminder of humanity's capacity for overreach and moral blindness. The Church's past confrontations with ideologies seeking to mold human perfection remind us that salvation lies not in genetic purity but in spiritual integrity.

The ethical dialogue surrounding genetic engineering is neither mono-dimensional nor simplistic. It encompasses considerations of justice, equality, and the potential for exploitation. The Church's moral teachings provide a scaffold on which these considerations must rest, urging us to look beyond the immediate allure of scientific triumphs to the broader societal and spiritual conundrums they engender.

The inherent dignity of every human person, as promulgated by Vatican II and articulated through subsequent papal encyclicals, stands as a bulwark against the commodification of human life. This principle finds itself at odds with any attempt to reduce human beings to mere collections of modifiable traits. The divine image impressed upon each individual forbids such reductionism and demands profound respect and cautious discernment.

Moreover, the Church's response to genetic engineering is undergirded by a profound affirmation of human liberty and the inviolability of conscience. These tenets are not antithetical to reason but rather are fulfilled within the harmonious integration of faith and reason. The teachings of the Church Fathers, like Saint Thomas Aquinas, advocate for an approach where free will is paramount, albeit guided by divine wisdom and moral law.

Ethical complexities arise, particularly when we consider genetic interventions in the embryonic state. Here, the Church's teachings on the sanctity of life from conception preclude any manipulative practices that undermine the inherent potential and dignity of the unborn. The manipulation of embryos for research, though tempting in its promise of medical marvels, falls foul of the principle that each human life, regardless of its stage, is sacrosanct.

Yet, as stewards of creation endowed with intellect and reason, humanity holds a dual responsibility: to harness the advances of science for the common good and to safeguard the sanctity of life ordained by the Creator. This dual mandate requires a prudential application of genetic engineering that aligns with the principles of justice, beneficence, and respect for human dignity.

Through pastoral letters, doctrinal teachings, and ethical exhortations, the Church offers a compass to navigate the turbulent waters of bioethical dilemmas. Not merely as a voice of caution but as a guiding light that emphasizes the inextricable link between technological advancement and moral responsibility. This is evident in documents like Donum Vitae and Dignitas Personae, which delineate the Church's stance on bioethical issues.

In sum, genetic engineering presents both an opportunity and a challenge, a test of our scientific prowess and our ethical mettle. The Church's response, anchored in a profound respect for human dignity and the sacredness of life, provides an essential corrective to the unfettered application of biotechnological innovations. It exhorteth us to ensure that our use of genetic knowledge remains ever within the bounds of moral responsibility and reverence for the divine image in which every human person is created.

This interplay between scientific discovery and human dignity is not merely a contemporary concern but is deeply rooted in the Church's timeless mission. As we look to the future, the Church's teachings will continue to serve as a moral lodestar, guiding humanity towards a more just and dignified application of genetic engineering, wherein the true essence of human worth is not lost amidst the fervor of scientific marvels.

Balancing Faith and Reason

In the grand tapestry of human dignity, the delicate act of balancing faith and reason emerges as a theme both timeless and urgent. The Church, in its wisdom, recognizes that scientific inquiry need not stand in opposition to divine revelation; rather, it beckons a harmonious dialogue where each illuminates the other. Faith cannot be reduced to mere superstition, nor can reason evolve into cold rationalism devoid of moral compass. It is in the symphony of these two where true human dignity finds its fullest expression. The Church's approach, as guided by long-standing tradition, emphasizes that ethical reflections on emerging technologies must be rooted in a worldview that upholds the sanctity and worth of every individual. The quest for knowledge, when aligned with faith, becomes not a mere pursuit of facts but a journey towards understanding our place in the divine order, reinforcing the inherent value bestowed upon us by our Creator.

The Church's Approach to Scientific Inquiry blossoms as a critical discourse within that grand chapter, "The Interplay Between Science and Human Dignity," uniquely intertwining with "Balancing Faith and Reason." In the labyrinthine corridors of human contemplation, where the paths of faith and reason converge, the Church's approach to scientific inquiry unfurls as a compass guiding believers through the complexities of modern scientific advancements.

From times ancient and hallowed, the Church has stood not as an adversary to scientific endeavors but as a staunch sentinel discerning the morality that must accompany such intellectual pursuits. The history of the Church reveals epochs where faith-filled scholars like Thomas Aquinas sought harmony between the divinely revealed truths and the empirical knowledge gleaned from the natural world. Such luminaries perceived no schism betwixt faith and reason but rather envisaged a divine tapestry wherein both threads wove together the splendor and boundless expanse of God's creation.

However, the Church's stance on scientific inquiry has often necessitated a delicate dance. The ecclesiastic authorities, conscious of their stewardship over the souls and minds of the faithful, have promulgated boundaries to ensure that the relentless quest for knowledge does not transgress the sacred demarcations of human dignity. This is not a curtailment of freedom but a safeguarding of it, illuminating the ethical horizons within which scientific endeavor must operate. Thus, the Church proposes not an autocratic dominion over scientific fields but a conscientious dialogue - a balance etched in the ink of moral theology and the blood of the martyrs of truth.

Employing a principle-based approach, the Church has espoused several guidelines for navigating the waters of scientific advancement. Limiting neither the imagination nor the curiosity inherent to human nature, these principles seek to invigorate a deeper understanding, ensuring that the pursuit of knowledge submits to the greater good of humanity. Herein lies the genuine crux of "Balancing Faith and Reason": upholding the dignity of the human person while aiding in the flourishing of scientific achievements.

Moreover, the Church's magisterium has incrementally issued statements, addressing emergent technologies and their ethical ramifications. Encyclicals and pastoral letters embody these insights, with figures such as Pope John Paul II articulating a vision wherein science and faith dance together in an unbroken circle. His encyclicals, "Fides et Ratio" (Faith and Reason) and "Evangelium Vitae" (The Gospel of Life), reflect an unwavering call for science to serve the true progress of the human person by adhering to ethical principles rooted in human dignity.

In juxtaposition, the Church's mentors, the Fathers and Doctors, have continuously engaged with scientific developments as a conduit to underscore God's hand in creation. These intellectual titans did not shy away from scientific discourse but rather embraced it as an opus of divine majesty. Augustine, Aquinas, and their successors fostered an environment wherein empirical inquiry was viewed as a divine mandate to explore the magnificence of the Creator's work.

It is undeniable that the contemporary Church possesses an ecclesial duty to adapt to an era where the scientific paradigm burgeons with dynamic advancements. This engendering epoch, teeming with breakthroughs in fields such as genetics, artificial intelligence, and biotechnology, propels the moral theologian to ponder the ethical dimensions spanning these frontiers. Embedded within "Balancing Faith and Reason," the Church's approach to these inquiries ensures that no innovation compromises the inherent sanctity bestowed upon human life.

Beyond the canonical decrees and philosophical expositions, we find the Church's educational institutions taking the helm in fostering scientific inquiry. Universities and research centers under ecclesiastical aegis flourish as bastions where the synthesis of faith and reason is not merely taught but lived. These institutions stand as testament to the Church's burgeoning commitment to advance scientific knowledge without abdicating the moral imperatives intrinsic to human dignity.

One must be cognizant, too, of the Church's role in cultivating a scientific ethos suffused with ethical reflection. Through seminars, publications, and interdisciplinary dialogues, ecclesial academicians elucidate the moral scaffolding necessary to harness scientific potential. Consultative bodies like the Pontifical Academy of Sciences represent the zenith of this mission, where theologians and scientists collaborate, seeking to map a conscientious trajectory for scientific inquiry.

In reflection, "The Church's Approach to Scientific Inquiry" is neither a dogmatic prescription nor an antagonistic reprimand but a loving exhortation. It aspires to usher humanity towards a future where scientific innovation and moral integrity converge harmoniously. Herein lies the quintessential interplay - the delicate equilibrium - epitomized in "Balancing Faith and Reason," envisioning a world where the pursuit of knowledge enhances, rather than erodes, the dignity of the human person.

To encapsulate, "The Church's Approach to Scientific Inquiry" within the grand theme of "Balancing Faith and Reason" beckons not the cessation of scientific exploration but its meticulous alignment with the divine ordinance of human dignity. It is the call to a noble pursuit where the intellect bears witness to the sacred worth of the human person, aligning every discovery with the transcendent value that faith upholds. In this sacred endeavor, the Church proclaims that true science and sound faith are not adversaries but allies in the celestial symphony of human dignity.

Ethical Guidelines for Emerging Technologies emerge as a paragon within the grand narrative of balancing faith and reason, forming the bedrock upon which our contemplation of The Interplay Between Science and Human Dignity relies. In the wake of relentless scientific advancement, humanity finds itself at a crossroads, where every innovation presents a dual-edged sword—capable of profound good or unsettling malevolence. Herein lies the necessity for a moral compass, a divine lodestar, to navigate these turbulent waters. The Catholic Church, steadfast in her mission to uphold the sanctity of the human person, stands as a beacon, illuminating the path for ethical deliberations concerning emerging technologies.

As we venture into the realms of genetic engineering and artificial intelligence, the Church's voice echoes with unwavering clarity, calling for discernment and prudence. Not every 'can' should necessarily translate to a 'should.' The potential to alter the very fabric of our being or to create autonomous entities capable of surpassing human intellect must be approached with reverence for the inherent dignity bestowed upon us by our Creator. This is not a mere philosophical exercise; it is a moral imperative grounded in the timeless teachings of the faith.

Consider the delicate matter of genetic manipulation. In the pursuit of eradicating hereditary diseases, the promise of CRISPR technology dazzles like a siren's song. Yet, the specter of eugenics, the bias towards 'designer babies,' and the reduction of human life to a mere product of engineering loom large. The Church's wisdom calls for a vigilant examination of both the ends and the means, ensuring that the sanctity of life is not sacrificed on the altar of progress.

Similarly, artificial intelligence, with its burgeoning capabilities, poses both marvel and menace. While algorithms can enhance human capacity and alleviate mundane toil, the Church reminds us that replacing human judgment, compassion, and ethical reasoning with cold arithmetic risks dehumanization. The dignity of the laborer, the value of personal interaction, and the irreplaceable worth of human intuition must guide our integration of AI into the societal fabric.

Guided by a profound respect for human dignity, the Church admonishes against the hubris of playing God. This admonition isn't a relic of antiquated thought but a cornerstone of ethical foresight. Technologies like cloning or brain-computer interfaces challenge not just our ethical boundaries but our understanding of what it means to be human. In these explorations, the Church demands a balance, a careful weighing of potential benefits against moral costs, always within the framework of an integrated human ecology.

Moreover, in fields like biotechnology, where the lines between treatment and enhancement blur, the Church advocates for a principle of humility. Technological prowess should not overshadow the profound mystery of human life. The interplay of chromosomes and neurons is not merely a puzzle to be solved but a divine tapestry woven with purpose and meaning. Thus, any intervention must honor this sacred order, lest we fall into the trap of mechanistic reductionism.

Furthermore, the Church holds a steady course against the commodification of human life. In the age of digital surveillance, data privacy issues, and the potential for biotechnological exploitation, ethical guidelines must underscore the inviolable dignity of each person. It is not enough to regulate technology; we must cultivate a culture where technology serves humanity and not the other way around. This is the harmonious dance of faith and reason—where innovation proceeds hand-in-hand with ethical responsibility, where progress is measured not merely in bytes and genes but in the upliftment of the human spirit.

In challenging contexts, such as stem cell research, the Church's stance is clear and resolute: the protection of life from conception to natural death is paramount. While adult stem cell research aligns with these principles, embryonic research ventures into morally perilous territory, as it involves the destruction of nascent human life. Herein, the Church's guidelines serve not as a barrier to scientific exploration but as a safeguard against ethical erosion. The message is unequivocal—life, in all its stages, is sacred and must be preserved with unfaltering resolve.

As we delve deeper into the digital age, data ethics becomes an overarching concern. The proliferation of digital identity, biometric markers, and cybernetic enhancements necessitates a robust ethical framework. The principles of transparency, consent, and the right to privacy are not just legal niceties but moral imperatives that reflect the Church's teaching on the dignity and freedom of the human person. Anonymity and security must be balanced with the need to prevent harm, ensuring that technological advancements are wielded not as tools of control but as instruments of empowerment.

The Catholic Church, with her rich heritage of moral teaching and intellectual tradition, implores us to maintain this delicate balance. Through the lens of faith, we see emerging technologies not as isolated phenomena but as integral to the broader narrative of human flourishing. Ethical guidelines for these technologies are thus not mere addendums but central to our understanding of progress. They're bridges between the empirical and the existential, the material and the spiritual.

In sum, the ethical guidelines for emerging technologies, as envisioned by the Church, provide a moral compass for navigating the thrilling yet treacherous terrains of scientific advancement. They call us to a higher standard, one that transcends utilitarian calculations and embraces the full spectrum of human dignity. This is the harmonious blend of faith and reason—a dialogical dance where each step forward is measured not only by technological prowess but by the depth of our commitment to the sanctity and worth of every human life.

Chapter 11: Personal Vocation and Human Dignity

In the grand tapestry of creation, woven with threads of divine intent, each individual's vocation stands as a testament to human dignity, a sacred call echoing from the dawn of existence. To fathom one's personal vocation is to embark on a pilgrimage of utmost gravity and grace, where the call to holiness intertwines with daily existence, affirming the innate worth bestowed by the Creator. Thus, in the discernment of one's vocation, there arises a reverence for the sanctity of human life, infusing mundane acts with profound significance. This journey is not solitary; it finds expression within the warmth of family and the embrace of community, where role models and saints illuminate the path. Therefore, in every heartbeat of vocation lived authentically, there lies an affirmation of the transcendent dignity of the human person, inviting both profound reflection and laudable action as decreed in moral teachings.

Understanding Personal Vocation

To grasp the profundity of personal vocation, one must first perceive it as an intimate call inscribed by the Divine Architect upon the human soul. It is not merely about one's occupation or temporal pursuits but rather an all-encompassing summons to holiness, framed by the eternal purposes of our Creator. This divine invitation beckons each individual to pursue a unique path that reflects both their intrinsic worth and their participation in the grand narrative of redemption. Consequently, the recognition and nurturing of one's personal vocation elevate the human spirit, harmonizing individual dignity with the greater glory of God. In this dance of sacred destiny and human endeavor, we discern the inextricable connection between divine calling and the inherent nobility bestowed upon every person, urging each to cultivate their gifts in service to both God and fellow man, thereby affirming the intrinsic sanctity of the human condition.

The Call to Holiness within the broader context of "Understanding Personal Vocation" occupies a most eminent position, transcending the mere academic or theological discourse and penetrating the very heart of human existence. Holiness, in its purest form, is neither an abstract ideal nor a distant goal attainable by a select few; it is the sublime vocation to which every soul is summoned. The divine call to sanctity whispers through the ages, echoing within the corridors of our conscience and inviting us to a transcendental union with the Almighty, where true dignity is realized in its fullest expression.

Our existence on this terrestrial plane is imbued with meaning not by the mere fact of our being but by the divine purpose interwoven in our creation. To grapple with the notion of personal vocation bereft of this call to holiness would be tantamount to envisioning a canvas void of its most vivid colors, rendering it dull and incomplete. Thus, the call to holiness is the lodestar guiding our earthly pilgrimage, directing our every step toward the realization of our ultimate nature.

But what is this "holiness" to which we are beckoned? Indeed, it is far from the simplistic notion of moral rectitude or pious observance of ritual. Holiness is the profound communion with the Divine, a state of being wherein the soul aligns itself with the will and love of God. It calls for the perfection of charity, an immersion in divine love that transforms and elevates our very essence. As we respond to this hallowed call, we partake in the divine life, shedding the fetters of sin and unfurling the wings of our true, God-given dignity.

Personal vocation, then, is inextricably linked to this divine summons. It is not a mere occupation or earthly duty but a unique mission engraved upon our souls by the Creator Himself. This mission is the pathway to holiness and, consequently, to our full human dignity. Each vocation, whether to marriage, consecrated life, or single-blessedness, presents a distinct avenue through which we may attain sanctity and achieve our full human potential.

Consider the diverse tapestry of human vocations: the clergy, who serve as shepherds to the flock, guiding souls towards eternal pasture; the laity, called to sanctify the world through the integration of faith and life; the consecrated virgins and religious, who live as eschatological signs of the Kingdom to come. Each vocation carries within it the seed of holiness, demanding a response of fidelity and love. By embracing our personal vocation with an ardent heart, we heed the divine call and embark on a journey towards the transcendent horizon of holiness.

The call to holiness is also an immense responsibility. It impels us to cultivate virtues, to shun the blandishments of vice, and to conform ourselves more keenly to the image and likeness of God. In doing so, we illuminate the path for others, becoming beacons of light amidst the encroaching shadows of a secular world. The practice of holiness, therefore, is not isolated but communal, affecting and inspiring our brothers and sisters towards their own sanctification.

Furthermore, this call encompasses the entirety of our being: mind, body, and spirit. It beckons us to integrate the intellectual, moral, and spiritual spheres of our lives. The pursuit of truth, goodness, and beauty converges in the person of Jesus Christ, the ultimate paragon of holiness. Engaging in continuous intellectual formation, moral rectitude, and spiritual depth draws us deeper into the mystery of Christ, the source and summit of all holiness.

Holiness, as the highest calling, births a profound respect for human dignity. In recognizing the call to holiness within ourselves, we are compelled to honor the same call within others. This mutual respect is the bedrock of true community, fostering love, justice, and peace. To deny any individual their dignity is to deny the very image of God imprinted upon them. Therefore, the call to holiness reinforces our commitment to uphold and defend the sanctity of every human life.

In conclusion, "The Call to Holiness" is a clarion call to all believers, resonating across the eons, urging us to transcend the mundane and embrace the divine. It is the essence of our personal vocation and the highest expression of our human dignity. By heeding this call, we participate in the divine economy of love and grace, contributing to the sanctification of ourselves and the world. Hence, let us respond with fervent hearts, undeterred by the trials of life, and ascend to the sublime heights of holiness, where our true dignity is eternally enshrined in the bosom of the Divine.

Vocational Discernment and Dignity finds itself nestled within the grand tapestry of understanding one's personal vocation, rooted in the inherent dignity granted to every human soul. Picture, if you will, the artisan sculpting from a raw block of marble a figure of exquisite grace. So too is the work of discerning one's vocation, a process of chiseling away the extraneous to reveal the divine masterpiece within.

The act of vocational discernment is not merely a superficial endeavor to ascertain a career path or life role. It is, rather, a sacred journey into the depths of one's being, where the call of the Divine whispers through the labyrinthine corridors of the soul. This journey is intertwined with the recognition of human dignity, for only through acknowledging the sacred worth imprinted upon us by the Creator can we truly understand the vocation to which we are called.

The ancient wisdom of the Church Fathers serves as a lamp unto our feet, illuminating the intricate connection between vocational discernment and human dignity. Saint Augustine, in his Confessions, eloquently speaks of the restlessness of the human heart until it finds rest in God. In a similar vein, the path of vocational discernment is a pilgrimage towards the tranquility that emerges from aligning one's life with the divine will. To discern one's vocation is to embrace the profound truth that each person, in their unique individuality, is called to reflect God's glory and to contribute to the tapestry of creation in a manner only they can.

Consider the perspective of Saint Thomas Aquinas, who elucidated the concept of the "ordo amoris," the order of love. To discern one's vocation is to order one's loves rightly, prioritizing divine love above all. This process necessitates a deep understanding of one's dignity as a being created in the image and likeness of God. Our choices, aspirations, and actions must all resonate with this divine image within us, leading us to a vocation that is not just a career, but a calling to holiness and service.

How does one embark upon this sacred journey of vocational discernment? The first step lies in prayer and contemplation, seeking the guidance of the Holy Spirit. Just as a mariner relies on the constellations to navigate the seas, so too must we rely on the divine light to guide us through the uncharted waters of our vocations. This is not a solitary endeavor, but one undertaken within the community of the faithful, supported by the wisdom of spiritual directors and the sacramental life of the Church.

Furthermore, the dignity of human personhood impels us to consider our vocational choices in the light of service to others. True vocational discernment transcends self-interest and seeks the good of the broader community. It calls us to examine how our unique gifts and talents can serve those around us, reflecting the love of Christ in a world often marred by selfishness and indifference. In this, we find the words of Pope Francis particularly poignant, as he urges the faithful to "go forth as a community of missionary disciples, each of us in our own way and all of us together."

It is imperative to approach vocational discernment with a sense of reverence for the inherent dignity of each human being. As we discern our call, we must also respect the vocations of others, acknowledging that each person's journey is a unique expression of the divine will. This mutual respect cultivates a culture of dignity where every person's vocation is celebrated and supported within the community of believers.

Notably, the vocational journey often encounters trials and uncertainties. These challenges, rather than diminishing our dignity, serve to refine and strengthen it. Through persevering in faith and trust, we embrace our identity as co-creators with God, participating in the unfolding of His divine plan. This perspective echoes the perennial teachings of the Church, affirming that human dignity is not dependent on external success or societal recognition but is rooted in our creation by God and our response to His call.

The relationship between personal vocation and human dignity is thus symbiotic, each enriching and informing the other. As we delve deeper into understanding our personal vocation, we concurrently gain a more profound appreciation of our intrinsic worth. Conversely, recognizing our dignity compels us to pursue our vocational call with greater fervor and commitment. This dynamic interplay fosters a life of purpose, fulfillment, and sanctity.

Finally, let us reflect upon how vocational discernment and dignity manifest in everyday life. Our personal vocations influence our interactions with family, community, and the broader society. When we live out our vocations authentically, our lives become a testament to the sanctity of all human life. In this way, we become living epistles, proclaiming the Gospel through our deeds and choices, upholding the truth that each person, in their vocational pursuit, mirrors the glory of the Creator.

In conclusion, vocational discernment is not merely a decision-making process but a profound journey into the heart of our identity and purpose, rooted in the unassailable dignity bestowed upon us by God. As we navigate this path with prayer, reflection, and communal support, we uncover the deepest truths of who we are and what we are called to be. In recognizing and embracing our personal vocations, we affirm the sacred worth of ourselves and others, contributing to a tapestry of divine beauty and grace that reflects the glory of our Creator.

Living Out Vocation in Everyday Life

The seamless integration of one's personal vocation into the quotidian rhythm of life manifests the profound dignity endowed upon the human person by the Creator. Each individual's calling, whether it be to the sacred bonds of matrimony, the celibate dedication of religious life, or the solitary path of singlehood, is not merely a pursuit confined to ecclesiastical realms but a continuous act of worship echoed through daily deeds. It is in the mundane and the monumental, from the tender care of a parent to the diligent labor of a professional, that personal vocation finds its fullest expression. The mundane duties we fulfill, uncelebrated and often unnoticed, are imbued with an eternal significance, transforming even the simplest of tasks into acts of divine accord. True adherence to one's vocation is a testament not of public grandeur but a silent, steadfast commitment to live out the Gospel's moral imperatives, reflecting the Church's timeless teachings and upholding the inviolable sanctity inherent in every human soul. Thus, the call to holiness intertwines with each moment, infusing the entirety of human existence with sacred purpose and reaffirming the ethos of human dignity.

Impacts on Family and Community As we enter the labyrinthine corridors of living out vocation in everyday life, we must examine the profound reverberations this has on family and community. In truth, the splendor of human dignity shines brightest not when cloistered in individualism but when expressed in its communal dimensions. How does the call to personal vocation extend beyond the self, seeking anchorage within familial bonds and the broader tapestry of communal life? This inquiry demands our careful contemplation.

First, consider the family, the smallest but most vital cell of societal structure. Herein, personal vocation first takes root, nourished by the soil of intimate relationships. The vocation of each family member, be it father, mother, child, or sibling, enriches this unit, creating a harmony of roles and responsibilities. As Thomas Aquinas might posit, the family is an organic unit that mirrors the divine order, where each participant contributes to the common good. By fulfilling their individual callings, family members affirm not only their worth but also the sanctity of those around them.

A father's vocation as a provider entails more than mere economic sustenance. It encompasses the moral and spiritual guidance he imparts to his children, thus weaving a tapestry of virtue and integrity. Similarly, a mother's vocation often intertwines the nurturing of physical life with the cultivation of the soul. Both roles, steeped in sacrifice and love, find their apex in the selfless service to one another, a microcosm of Christ's love for His Church. Thus, the dignity of personal vocation enhances familial bonds, rendering them emblematic of divine grace.

Children, in their formative years, thrive in environments where vocations are not just spoken of but lived out authentically. Witnessing their parents' adherence to their callings, children learn the language of discernment and commitment. They absorb the values of perseverance and integrity, laying the groundwork for their future vocations. The family, therefore, becomes a crucible where human dignity is molded, tested, and ultimately perfected.

The broader community also reflects the luminous impact of personal vocation. When individuals fulfill their callings, they contribute to the common wealth of society. A carpenter who takes pride in his craft, a teacher who inspires with wisdom, or a doctor who heals with compassion, each exemplifies the dignity of labor and the sanctity of fulfilling one's role in the grand design. In this shared endeavor, the community becomes a living testament to human dignity, a collective witnessing to the divine order.

Indeed, the Church teaches that human dignity is intertwined with the concept of the common good. As St. John Paul II elucidated, the dignity of the individual person must always consider the relational aspect of existence. In other words, our vocation is not solely for our benefit but is intricately linked to the well-being of others. This relational aspect finds its most vivid expression within the community, a web of interdependencies reflecting the divine will.

However, let us not romanticize this ideal; the practical realities of living out vocation can be arduous. The challenges faced by families and communities are many, from economic hardships to moral dilemmas. It is in these crucibles that the true measure of human dignity is tested and, by the grace of God, often triumphs. Through these trials, the steadfastness of one's vocation becomes a beacon of hope and resilience for others, illuminating the path through shared struggles.

Moreover, personal vocations can sometimes clash with communal needs, creating a tension that requires careful navigation. Modern sociological insights remind us that while individual fulfillment is essential, it must harmonize with collective responsibilities. This balance, intricate as it is, underscores the need for a discerning heart and a willingness to place others above self when necessary. The Church's moral teachings provide invaluable guidance here, emphasizing the virtue of charity as the highest form of living out one's vocation.

Community living also offers a rich array of role models, figures who embody their vocations with such fidelity that they inspire others to do the same. Saints within the community, heralds of faith in action, serve as tangible exemplars of how to live out vocation with dignity and grace.

Their lives are a testament to the transformative power of vocation, extending its influence far beyond personal satisfaction to communal upliftment.

Additionally, the community serves as a support system, offering encouragement and resources for individuals striving to live out their vocations. From parish groups to neighborhood associations, these frameworks provide a nurturing environment where vocations can flourish. The Church plays a pivotal role in fostering such communities, emphasizing the principles of solidarity and subsidiarity to empower individuals within their local contexts.

Importantly, living out vocation within family and community fosters a culture of respect and understanding. It serves as a constant reminder that every person is a reflection of the divine image, deserving of dignity and honor. Such a culture mitigates the alienation often found in secular settings, replacing it with a sense of belonging and mutual respect. This communal affirmation of dignity becomes a bulwark against the dehumanizing forces of modernity.

Moreover, personal vocation, when rooted in the family and expanded into the community, holds the potential for social transformation. It becomes a catalyst for ethical behavior, fostering environments where justice and compassion prevail. This transformative power, coupled with the Church's moral teachings, can bring about substantial social change, addressing issues of inequality and injustice with a rooted sense of human dignity.

The significance of living out vocation within a community extends even to the smallest acts of daily life. Simple gestures of kindness, inspired by one's vocation, have a ripple effect, touching countless lives in profound ways. These acts collectively build a strong foundation for a community grounded in dignity and respect. It's a call to transcend the self, to see vocation as a shared journey toward a higher purpose.

In conclusion, the sacred interplay between personal vocation and the spheres of family and community unveils the multifaceted splendor of human dignity. In these intimate and collective arenas, the dignity of the human person finds its fullest expression and greatest fulfillment. Such a harmonious existence not only affirms the sanctity of life but also elevates the collective human experience, drawing it ever closer to the divine ideal. In this, the essence of the Church's teachings on human dignity is robustly manifested, guiding us toward a life of purpose, interconnectedness, and divine grace.

Role Models and Saints dwell as luminescent guides within the grand tapestry of "Personal Vocation and Human Dignity." As we shepherd the spirit and elevate the calling, these exalted figures illumine the pathway of our everyday existence. Saints, having etched their sacred stories upon the annals of time, endow us with paradigms of sanctity and virtue; hence, they become the very sinew of our moral and spiritual life. It is through the prism of their lives that we perceive our own potential for holiness, alike a sculptor discerning form within unhewn marble.

In the ordinariness of everyday life, we seek to embody the virtues of these venerable persons; their tales of faith and perseverance whisper to us amidst the most trifling tasks. Consider the sanctified life of Saint Francis of Assisi, who embraced poverty to enrich his soul with the virtues of humility and charity. His devotion speaks to us as we navigate a world abounding in materialism, reminding us that the true measure of a person lies not in their possessions but in their capacity for love and self-giving. His life, a mosaic of simplicity and abnegation, becomes a beacon illuminating the essence of human dignity, attained through surrender to divine calling.

Equally illustrious is Saint Teresa of Calcutta, whose relentless care for the poorest of the poor stands as a testimony to the human spirit's resilience and capacity for compassion. Her actions teach us that living out our vocation means to serve with fervent love those whom society casts aside. Every encounter with the marginalized thus metamorphosed into an encounter with Christ, affirming that every human being bears the imprint of the divine. Her life becomes a clarion call to mindful service and an unyielding reminder that dignity is an intrinsic quality, irrespective of social status or circumstance.

Imagine further, the resolute faith of Saint Thomas More, whose unwavering adherence to conscience, even unto death, exalts the vital interplay between personal vocation and moral integrity. His martyrdom reveals the cost of discipleship and the supreme dignity in adhering to one's convictions against societal pressures. His life offers profound insights about the sanctity of the human person as a moral agent who stands before divine judgement, undeterred by temporal consequences.

Within the sanctified tableau of our Redeemed, the Blessed Virgin Mary appears as the paragon of obedience and grace. Her Fiat – "Be it done unto me according to thy word" – encapsulates the quintessence of vocational acceptance and human dignity. Upon our daily crossroads and decisions, we glance toward her example, recognizing a profound humility harmonized with divine exaltation. Her life is an indelible testament to the serene power of consent to Divine Will, thus infusing our own vocational discernment with both courage and submission to God's providence.

Through the venerated mosaic of these saints, we discern a pattern of divine love and service that transcends the mere details of their lives, weaving a larger narrative of communal benefit and personal sanctification. As we strive to fulfill our vocations, the saints' lives offer tangible illustrations of how to balance duties towards family, community, and God. Their chronicles of trials and triumphs furnish us with a repository of wisdom that becomes quintessential in navigating our spiritual journeys.

Equally enthralling is the life of Saint Augustine of Hippo, whose intellectual rigour and poignant confessions guide us through the labyrinth of human frailty and divine grace. His transformative journey from a life mired in hedonism to one enraptured by divine love stands as an eloquent witness to the transformative power of divine grace. The probing depths of his writings awaken in us a profound awareness of our own weaknesses and the redeeming power of God's love, thus enriching our understanding of human dignity rooted in divine mercy.

In the humble obscurity of clerics like Saint John Vianney, we encounter a relentless dedication to pastoral care and the unassuming power of sanctity. His ministry, deeply rooted in the everyday rhythms of parish life, reminds us that fulfilling our vocation does not necessitate grand gestures, but rather, a faithful adherence to daily duties performed with love and devotion. His life, abounding in simple acts of kindness and piety, casts a bright light on the profound impacts of vocational fidelity in the common spheres of life.

Conversing silently with the heart, these lives of saints whisper eternal truths amidst our daily vocations. They stand before us as living epistles, written not with ink but with the Spirit of the living God, on tablets of human hearts. The hallowed lives of these illustrious figures render the abstract notions of human dignity tangible and incumbent upon our own endeavors. They become living testaments to the inexorable link between personal vocation and human dignity, urging us to emulate their virtues in the quotidian details of our lives.

In closing, we must recognize that the saints are not distant idols but empathetic companions on our own spiritual journeys. Their lives, rich in both divine mystery and human experience, teach us that our vocation is a holy endeavor, imbued with the dignity that comes from being created in the image of God. As we navigate the labyrinth of our daily lives, let the saints be our compass, always pointing towards the ineffable light of divine love and dignity.

Chapter 12: The Future of Human Dignity and Moral Teaching

As we traverse the ever-unfolding tapestry of modernity, the bedrock of human dignity finds itself besieged by the tempestuous winds of secularism and the relentless evolution of globalization. The Church must gird herself, not with steel but with the immutable truths enshrined in centuries of moral teaching, to stand as a bulwark against this tide. It is her solemn charge to illuminate the path through the encroaching darkness, ensuring that the immutable worth of every human soul does not wither into the annals of forgetfulness. This noble quest calls for an ardent dedication to fostering education and awareness, crafting initiatives that weave respect and an intrinsic appreciation for human dignity into the very fabric of society. Thus, the Church will continue to sculpt a cosmos where human dignity is not merely a whispered ideal but a resounding anthem that guides every action and thought. In this hallowed mission, she beckons all who cherish the sacredness of the human person to join her in erecting a future where moral clarity dispels the shadows, and dignity blossoms unchained from the fetters of the ephemeral and the transient.

Challenges in the Modern World

As the tapestry of our age unfolds, the pillars of human dignity and moral teaching confront adversities unprecedented in scope and complexity. The stormwinds of secularism blow fiercely, seeking to erode the divine worth intrinsic to every soul, while the relentless march of globalization presents a mosaic of ethical dilemmas, demanding our prudence and sagacity. In the cacophony of competing ideologies, the sanctity of life is oft besieged, and the perennial truths of the Church are challenged by transient doctrines of convenience. Yet, in this trial by fire, the call to uphold the immutable principles of human dignity resounds with urgency. The task before us is Herculean, yet in our steadfast adherence to the moral compass provided by our faith, we find the fortitude to navigate these tumultuous seas. Thus, as we grapple with the moral quandaries of our epoch, we must anchor our resolve in the eternal, perpetuating the luminous teachings of our heritage amidst the shadows of modernity.

Secularism and Human Dignity finds itself ensnared in a paradox, as it bids us revel in the liberties of modern life while neglecting the sacred intrinsic worth bestowed upon man by divine grace. In truth, the modern world, riddled with secularist ideologies, relentlessly challenges the very substratum of human dignity laid down by centuries of theological and philosophical meditation. To comprehend the vast implications of this struggle, we must delve into the corridors of history, ascertain the present perils, and envision the prospects for moral teaching in a decidedly secular age.

Secularism, with its clarion call of separation from religious authority, often purports to offer a realm of neutrality, where freedom and progress bloom unaided by spiritual guidance. Yet, this autonomy can dehumanize, dismembering the soul from man's corporeal existence. As the sword of secularism cleaves the sacred from the profane, it rends the metaphysical fabric that cloaks human dignity. Without acknowledgement of a higher power, man risks becoming naught but a mere cog in the machinery of society, devoid of the grandeur and purpose that faith enkindles.

Consider the philosophical roots from whence secularism springs. It boasts an exaltation of human reason and empirical evidence, eschewing what it deems superstitious constructs of the divine. While such commitments have propelled humanity into an age of scientific and economic marvels, they seldom grapple with the metaphysical questions that ennoble mankind. In this stark landscape, human dignity is often relegated to a social construct, mutable at the whims of cultural tides rather than anchored in the immutable truths of divine creation.

Within the sphere of moral teachings, secularism assails the Church's doctrines that shield human worth. By undermining the sanctity of life, the integrity of marriage, and the intrinsic value each soul possesses, secular ideologues inadvertently propagate a utilitarian ethic, where human beings are valued based on their utility rather than their God-given dignity. A distressing manifestation of such a worldview can be perceived in bioethical debates, where matters of life and death are adjudicated more by pragmatic considerations than moral imperatives, thus threatening the inalienable dignity each person carries from conception to natural death.

As the ordinations of secularism infiltrate the domains of education, media, and governance, society often finds itself adrift in a sea of moral relativism. The Church, henceforth, prepares to navigate these treacherous waters, reaffirming the eternal precepts that sustain human dignity even in the face of temporal change. Our moral theologians must articulate, with the fervor of the prophets, the indispensable connection between faith and dignity. Man, after all, is created imago Dei, in the image of God, a truth that transcends the fleeting propositions of secular dogma.

The perils confronting human dignity in a secularized society are not without historical antecedents. Throughout epochs of enlightenment and renaissance, thinkers constantly grappled with balancing secular knowledge and divine wisdom. Yet, it is in these dialogues that the Church finds solace, for history bears witness to the resilience of faith and the enduring nature of divine truth. Contemporary sociologists and moral philosophers must hence examine these periods, drawing lessons that might illumine our present and guide our future.

Indeed, secularism does present opportunities for the Church to demonstrate the universal applicability of its teachings. Balancing unwavering fidelity to doctrine with an understanding of the modern secular mind can allow the Church to voice its timeless message afresh. The challenges posed by secularism can thereby be transformed into a clarion call for deeper catechesis, community engagement, and advocacy that underscores the sacredness inherent in each person, regardless of societal status or function.

Furthermore, the Church must harness the tools of modernity to combat the encroaching tide of secularism. Utilizing the very advancements in communication, technology, and social organization that secular ideologies often claim as their own, the Church can fortify the ramparts of human dignity. Through initiatives in social media, education, and community organization, the Church can promulgate its message of dignity robustly and effectively, ensuring it resonates within the hearts of the faithful and the uncertain alike.

Moreover, the interplay between secular governance and human dignity must be scrutinized. While secular states purport to uphold democratic freedoms, true liberty is inextricably linked with moral responsibility. Without the guiding hand of divine law, secular statutes can inadvertently foster environments where human dignity is compromised in favor of convenience or expedience. The Church's moral teachings serve as an indispensable counterbalance, emphasizing that authentic freedom arises from adherence to moral truth and the inherent values that stem from divine creation.

To safeguard human dignity amidst the currents of secularism, collaboration between the Church and secular institutions must be pursued judiciously, building bridges where possible but with unwavering fidelity to the doctrines that uphold the sacred worth of every human being. By engaging in dialogue, seeking common ground, and fostering understanding, the Church can witness to the transformative power of faith and its pivotal role in safeguarding human dignity.

In summation, **Secularism and Human Dignity** remain entangled in a grand dialectic, a clash that reveals the stakes of modernity while reaffirming the perennial truths of faith. As the lanterns of secular thought shine brightly, casting shadows that often obscure the divine, the Church must illuminate the path with the enduring light of its teachings. Thus, the sanctity of human dignity, far from being an archaic relic, emerges as the very essence of humane coexistence, demanding recognition and reverence in every age and clime.

Let this be the clarion call to our moral theologians, sociologists, and faithful believers. The defense of human dignity against the forces of secularism is not merely a task for today but a mission spanning the epochs. As we traverse this challenging landscape, may we be bolstered by the wisdom of our forebears and the enduring truths of our faith, steadfast in the belief that every human being, imbued with divine worth, remains the crown of creation, deserving of unassailable dignity.

Globalization and Ethical Considerations encompass myriad complexities that thrust the concept of human dignity and moral teachings into both luminous and problematic realms. In an era where the conflux of cultures, ideologies, and philosophies transpires with unprecedented rapidity, the challenges to preserving the sanctity and inalienable dignity of the human person grow exceedingly intricate.

As the boundaries of nations dissolve into the nebulous expanse of a globalized world, the ethical predicates set forth by the Catholic Church encounter both novel opportunities and vigorous challenges. To fathom the implications of globalization upon human dignity, one must first delve into the torrential confluence of cultural currents that define our epoch. Therein lies both promise and peril, for while globalization can indeed serve as a conduit for the universal recognition of human worth, it equally augments the risk of ethical relativism and moral disintegration.

The rapid interchange of goods, ideas, and people across global frontiers engenders manifold ventures for the propagation of Catholic moral teachings. On the one hand, globalization facilitates the dissemination of the Church's message to far-flung regions, allowing the tenets of human dignity to be grafted onto diverse cultural landscapes. The universality of the Church's moral teachings finds new resonance as it traverses the worldly plane, engaging with varied cultures and bringing to fore the perennial truths that transcend temporal boundaries.

Conversely, the relentless march of globalization harbors the latent hazard of fostering a homogenized ethos that may overlook the profound multiplicity inherent in human cultures. Ethical considerations become critical as the Church endeavors to navigate through a milieu where secularist notions and materialistic values often seek to dilute the sanctified perception of the human person. Herein lies the exigency to assert the immutable principles that underpin Catholic moral teachings amidst the cacophony of competing global ideologies.

The ethical quandaries of globalization call upon moral theologians to reconcile the exigencies of a connected world with the uncompromising dignity bestowed upon every human soul by virtue of divine image. It becomes essential to resist the commodification of the human person, which globalization's market-driven dynamics might inadvertently encourage. The intrinsic worth of the human being must not be subsumed under the utilitarian calculus of profit and efficiency that often dictates global transactions.

Moreover, globalization brings to the fore the stark disparities in wealth, health, and opportunity that persist across the world's regions. The moral theologian must grapple with the ethical imperatives of addressing these inequities, fostering an advocacy rooted in the Church's preferential option for the poor. Ensuring that the human dignity of marginalized populations is not eroded by the tides of global economic forces requires active engagement and an unwavering commitment to social justice.

One must also consider the ramifications of technological advancements, which are often accelerated by globalization. Biotechnological innovations, artificial intelligence, and digital interconnectivity pose profound ethical questions pertaining to human dignity. The Church is called to offer guidance that harmonizes the benefits of technological progress with the moral imperatives that safeguard the sanctity of human life. This entails a discerning approach that both embraces scientific advancements and critically appraises their ethical ramifications.

Further, the Church's doctrinal stance on the family unit as the cornerstone of society faces both challenges and opportunities in a globalized context. The migratory movements facilitated by globalization can either fracture familial bonds or create new communal solidarities. It is incumbent upon the Church to emphasize the enduring moral and social value of the family, advocating for policies that reinforce familial integrity and uphold the dignity of each family member.

Thus, as globalization reshapes the modern world, ethical considerations burgeon in complexity. The Church's teachings on human dignity must be articulated with renewed vigor, addressing both the microcosmic spheres of individual lives and the macrocosmic currents of global phenomena. The articulation must strive to transcend cultural barriers, delivering a message that is both universally relevant and deeply rooted in the Church's timeless moral tradition.

The task before us is formidable; it demands a nuanced understanding of the multiplicity of challenges engendered by globalization and an unwavering commitment to the moral principles that uphold human dignity. The Church's advocacy must be both principled and pragmatic, eschewing moral relativism while engaging constructively with the diverse ethical landscapes of the globalized world.

In conclusion, as the specter of globalization continues to cast its influence far and wide, the ethical bedrock of human dignity must remain unshaken. The Church's moral teachings provide the compass by which to navigate this intricate terrain, ensuring that the intrinsic worth of every person is recognized, respected, and cherished. By steadfastly championing human dignity, amidst the multifaceted challenges wrought by globalization, the Church affirms its timeless mission to uphold the sacredness of the human person in all its divine splendor.

The Church's Role in Future Advocacy

The Church, as custodian of eternal truths and moral teachings, must gird itself for the burgeoning challenges that besiege the dignity of human life in the modern epoch. In a world swept by the tempest of secularism and the tides of globalization, the Church's clarion call to uphold and advocate for human worth becomes ever more imperative. Guided by Scripture and the time-hallowed wisdom of the Fathers, the Church must actively engage in crafting initiatives aimed at education and awareness, thus fortifying the faithful against the insidious encroachments upon human sanctity. With the steadfast resolve of a beacon in the dark, the Church is tasked with building a culture steered by respect and dignity, where each soul is acknowledged, cherished, and elevated, reflecting the divine image inherent within. Such advocacy is not mere reaction but a prophetic witnessing, heralding a future where moral clarity and human dignity prevail amidst an increasingly fractured world.

Initiatives for Education and Awareness shall be the cornerstone thesis in the grand canvas titled *"The Church's Role in Future Advocacy."* In an era defined by volatile mores and burgeoning secularism, the ecclesiastical community must wield its venerable faculties to enlighten and educate, thereby upholding the sanctity of human dignity.

First and foremost, hitherto the bastions of knowledge, such as seminaries and theological institutes, must augment their curricula. Incorporating comprehensive teachings on human dignity and moral theology, sessions should include both ancient wisdom and contemporary quandaries. It is by this holistic approach that we shall enlighten future clerics, enabling them to grapple efficaciously with the complexities of modern life. Indeed, the weighty tomes of Aquinas and Augustine must share their sacred shelves with the moral imperatives of the present age.

The edification of the laity stands no less crucial. Catechetical programs, traditionally reservoirs of faith's fundamentals, should now encompass exhaustive expositions on human dignity. Weekly homilies ought to reverberate moral teachings, skillfully woven into the fabric of everyday life. For verily, it is through this incessant persuasion and cultivation of conscience that the faithful wings to an understanding of their inviolable worth, which is but a reflection of the divine.

To galvanize broader societal recognition and acceptance of human dignity, the Church should immerse itself in the digital realm. By utilizing technology—social media platforms, online forums, and virtual courses—the Church can reach a vast audience, especially the youth. The younger generation, often buffeted by errant winds of modernity and moral relativism, craves guidance steeped in authentic wisdom. Through compelling digital content and interactive sessions, the Church can engage, educate, and embolden the young to walk the righteous path.

Furthermore, ecclesiastical bodies should orchestrate symposia, conferences, and public lectures. These forums can be open to not just believers, but also to philosophers, scientists, and sociologists. The cross-pollination of ideas from varied fields would render a robust defense of human dignity. By instituting such platforms, the Church declares its readiness to engage with the world in dialogue, unafraid to defend and propagate its moral convictions.

The value of partnerships with educational institutions can scarce be exaggerated. Schools and universities, even those beyond the traditional Catholic purview, must be targeted for collaborative initiatives. Guest lectures, workshops, and discourse sessions aimed at elucidating the Church's stance on human dignity can serve as vital levers. Bringing young minds face-to-face with Catholic moral thought instills an appreciation for human dignity that transcends denominational lines.

No educational initiative should be devoid of community outreach. Parishes can act as the nuclei of localized education and awareness campaigns. Programs aimed at youth groups, family support systems, and community action guilds will create ripples far beyond the church walls. By taking the teachings into homes and streets, the Church reinforces its unwavering commitment to the dignity of every soul.

In regions with restricted access to formal education, particularly in impoverished or politically unstable areas, the Church's role must be that of both educator and liberator. Mobile schools, community learning centers, and clandestine study groups can clandestinely foster a culture of respect and dignity. Resources in local languages and dialects, coupled with culturally sensitive pedagogical approaches, shall ensure that the message resonates deeply.

Monsignor, bishops, and even the papal voice itself must lend their influence towards public awareness campaigns. Statements, encyclicals, and apostolic exhortations can serve as moral clarion calls, uniting the faithful worldwide. Such documents, when disseminated broadly, can galvanize the Church's global constituency, igniting a collective fervor for upholding human dignity.

Additionally, the laity must be encouraged to pursue life choices and careers that reflect and magnify the teachings on human dignity. Whether in medicine, law, education, or social work, their vocational pursuits ought to breathe life into the Church's moral doctrines. Role models and exemplary figures, both historical and contemporary, should be spotlighted as beacons guiding this noble quest.

Upon this edifice of education and awareness, the Church must enshrine a culture of perpetual inquiry and adaptation. With each new moral dilemma that emerges, the institution must stand ready to refine its pedagogical approaches. This agile mindset would ensure that the teachings remain relevant, resonant, and rooted in unassailable truth.

In solemn contemplation, let us thus envision a future where every man, woman, and child, regardless of their station, comprehends their inherent worth—a worth underscored by divine ordination and echoed through centuries of moral teaching. Through these educational initiatives, unwavering and omnipresent, the Church can reawaken the world to the transcendental value of human dignity.

Building a Culture of Respect and Dignity In charting the course for the future of human dignity and moral teaching, the role of the Church stands as a beacon amidst the torrents of modernity. The endeavor to foster a culture of respect and dignity is not merely a noble aspiration but a divine mandate that necessitates both action and contemplation.

Engraved in the very heart of the Church's teachings, human dignity is not a distant ideal or abstract principle. It is a tangible reality, proclaimed by the birth of every child and affirmed by the lives of saints and martyrs. The Church must, with fervor and steadfastness, elevate the understanding of this fundamental truth to the societies it seeks to transform.

The creation of this culture must begin with education. Education is not confined to the walls of academia but extends into the fabric of everyday life. It is in the catechesis of the young, the preaching to congregations, and the lived example of virtue displayed by the faithful. The Church must seize every opportunity to articulate and demonstrate the intrinsic worth of the human person, endowed with dignity by the Creator.

Consider, then, the formation of conscience as a cornerstone of this cultural edifice. The conscience, properly enlightened by grace and Church teaching, discerns the sanctity of each human being, irrespective of status or circumstance. This formation must be continuous, adapting to the complexities of contemporary moral dilemmas while remaining rooted in eternal truths.

Moreover, the Church must champion social advocacy to build this culture of respect. In addressing the plights and injustices faced by the marginalized, the Church illustrates the principles of charity and justice. This advocacy must be bold and unwavering, addressing systemic issues with solutions grounded in the teachings of Christ and the social doctrine of the Church.

Let the Church not forget the power of dialogue in cultivating respect. Engaging with the broader society, including those who hold divergent views, fosters a mutual understanding that can break down barriers of prejudice and ignorance. Through dialogue, respect is not only taught but exemplified, showing the world a model of humility and charity.

The Eucharist itself serves as a profound testament to this culture of dignity. In the sacrament, the faithful encounter the Real Presence of Christ, a mystery that underscores the value He places on humanity by becoming one with us. The reverence and solemnity with which the Eucharist is celebrated remind the Church and the world of the sacredness of human life.

Furthermore, consider the role of the laity in these endeavors. Laypersons, in their quotidian vocations, hold the potential to influence and transform society from within. Their witness, in marketplaces, workplaces, and homes, weaves the principles of the Church into the daily rhythms of life, creating a symphony of respect and dignity that resonates through each community.

Parishes and dioceses must also engage in concerted efforts to create programs and initiatives that embody these values. Whether through workshops, retreats, or service projects, these practical applications serve as scaffolding to the grand structure of a culture that venerates human dignity.

The challenges are undoubtedly great, particularly in an age where secularism and relativism often obscure the inherent worth of the individual. Yet, these challenges only magnify the imperative and glory of the Church's mission. Each effort, each act of kindness, each affirmation of dignity contributes to an edifice that stands as a testament to the enduring truth of the human person's worth.

Leaders within the Church must be courageous and visionary, embracing new methods of communication and outreach to convey the timeless message. They must employ technology and media to spread the teachings of dignity, ensuring that the message reaches every corner of the globe, from bustling cities to secluded hamlets.

Lastly, prayer and sacramentality underpin the entire enterprise. It is through grace, accessed in prayer and the sacraments, that the Church derives its strength and efficacy. A culture of respect and dignity must be bathed in prayer, invoking the Holy Spirit's guidance and blessing on each endeavor.

Hence, "Building a Culture of Respect and Dignity" is not an ephemeral aspiration but a divine calling that the Church must heed with great devotion and zeal. The future beckons with both promise and peril, but with unwavering commitment to the dignity of the human person, the Church can illuminate the path toward a more just, loving, and respectful world.

Conclusion

As we draw our discourse to a close, it becomes imperative to bathe in the light of our collective deliberations and weigh the formidable forces of human dignity and the moral tenets heralded by the Church. Through the intertwining of scriptural mandates, theological reflections, philosophical musings, and the unwavering moral guidance bestowed upon us by the Church, we stand before a luminous portrait of the human person, sanctified and noble, amidst the frailty of mortal coils.

The gravitas of understanding the sacrosanctity of human dignity stems not merely from an acknowledgment of inherent worth but from an embrace of the ontological truth; that each person is a reflection of the Divine Image. Such an understanding prompts reverence and invokes an ethical symphony whereby our actions are harmonized with the Creator's will. It is the infallible echo of Augustine and Aquinas, reverberating through the corridors of time, that consecrates our identity and fortifies our moral compass.

Our exploration embarked on the ancient pathways of Scripture, where the prophets and apostles collectively affirmed the intrinsic value and worthiness of the human person. Through both Old and New Testament exegesis, we distilled the essence of what it means to be created in the Imago Dei, culminating in the recognition of every soul's inviolable dignity. The resonance of these sacred texts continues to pulsate through our collective conscience, unwavering and steadfast.

Theological voices, from the august Church Fathers to the conciliar decrees of Vatican II, have illustrated with profound clarity the immutable doctrine of human personhood and worth. The Church, as a vigilant guardian of truth, has persistently championed a narrative steeped in the sanctity and sacredness of every human life. In this light, theological reflections become the pillars upon which we stand, stabilizing our ethical endeavors and moral pursuits.

Philosophical foundations, ardently explored through the lens of Aristotle's reasoning and Stoic meditations, augment our theological insights with rigorous intellectual stewardship. The classical and contemporary philosophies converge, offering an enriched tapestry of human dignity that deepens our comprehension and fortifies our convictions. This philosophical contemplation is a testament to the timeless quest for truth and moral rectitude.

Furthermore, the moral teachings of the Church furnish us with textured guidance — from the Decalogue's divine prescriptions to the comprehensive moral elucidations found within the Catechism. These teachings inform and transform us, not merely as directives but as a living moral tradition that shapes our conduct and aligns our wills with divine purpose. The ethical implications bear practical fruit, influencing our decisions in bioethics and social justice, a testament to our unwavering commitment to uphold life's sanctity at every stage.

The apologia for human dignity is not solely a proclamation but an articulate defense, grounded in reason and faith. Scriptural apologetics and rational discourse equip us to face contemporary challenges and counter any denigration of human worth with robust, reasoned arguments. This intellectual and spiritual bulwark ensures that the sanctity of human life remains an unassailable truth.

In traversing the terrains of life's ethical dimensions, the Church's teachings on abortion, euthanasia, and the care for the elderly and vulnerable underscore our dedication to safeguarding life. Each policy and principle serves as a beacon, guiding us toward compassionate, life-affirming choices. This reverence for life resonates through the ages, a clarion call to honor every breath from conception to natural death.

Social justice, as illumined by Catholic social teaching, calls us to a conscientious solidarity with the marginalized and a resolute advocacy for the common good. The historical and modern applications of these principles reflect a Church engaged in the world, striving to cultivate a society wherein dignity and justice are not mere ideals but living realities. Our moral responsibility extends beyond personal piety to a collective endeavor to uplift and protect the least among us.

The endowment of conscience, invigorated by grace and free will, acts as our intimate guide in moral decision-making. It is through the prudent formation and education of conscience that we navigate the labyrinth of ethical dilemmas with integrity and fidelity to divine law. Every decision, whether mundane or complex, becomes a testament to our moral integrity, reflecting our deepest commitments and highest aspirations.

In the realm of human rights, the Church's teachings align sacred truths with secular aspirations, traversing the chasm between divine ordinances and contemporary human rights discourse. These teachings provide a moral framework that confronts modern challenges, calling for a harmonious reimagining of rights in the light of divine justice and mercy.

The interplay between scientific discovery and human dignity emerges as a dynamic dialogue where faith and reason coalesce. Advances in medical science and emerging technologies challenge us to integrate ethical wisdom with scientific progress. The Church's balanced approach ensures that the sanctity of human life is preserved amidst the rapid evolution of knowledge and capability.

Personal vocation, discerned through prayer and reflection, becomes a sacred avenue through which human dignity is actualized. Whether through familial roles, community involvement, or emulation of saintly lives, our vocational pursuits reflect our unique participation in the divine mission. This vocational fidelity enhances communal life and manifests the beauty of God's creation in diverse and meaningful ways.

The future of human dignity and moral teaching lies within our grasp, contingent upon our response to the modern world's challenges. Secularism, globalization, and ethical conundrums may obscure the path, but the Church's unwavering advocacy for dignity invites us to respond with courage and conviction. Initiatives for education and awareness are vital to building a culture that esteems and respects every human person.

In summation, the stately edifice of human dignity, buttressed by the moral teachings of the Church, stands as an enduring testament to the sanctity of life. Our collective journey through scripture, theology, philosophy, and moral teaching reveals a composite truth, a mosaic of divine and human latitude. Let us, as stewards of this profound mystery, ever strive to honor the inviolable dignity bestowed upon us, weaving our lives into a resplendent tapestry of sanctity and grace.

Appendix A: Appendix

In the gathering twilight of this tome, we present unto thee an assemblage of pivotal documents and resources, a veritable treasury for those who seek to delve deeper into the profound discourse on human dignity and moral theology as expounded by the Church. Within this hallowed collection, one shall find the sagacious proclamations of august councils, the venerable writings of Church Fathers, and the monumental encyclicals that have indelibly marked the annals of moral philosophy. These texts stand not merely as relics of an archaic past but resonate with the clarion call of eternal truths, ever timely and eternally pertinent. Herein, every moral theologian, Roman Catholic, and sociologist may glean the wisdom needed to undergird the sacredness of the human person, ensuring that the light of divine moral precepts continues to illuminate the path of humanity. May this appendix serve as both a beacon and bastion for those devoted to safeguarding the ineffable dignity of every soul.

Key Documents and Resources

The axioms and tenets enumerated within this tome emanate from a rich tapestry of documents, wherein sacred tradition intertwines with divine revelation. Such a confluence presents a bedrock upon which the intrinsic worth of the human person is etched indelibly. The source materials shall hence be unveiled for the avid scholar and devoted theologue, offering both a beacon of guidance and a reservoir of wisdom.

Foremost amongst these seminal texts stands the Holy Bible, the authoritative scripture encompassing the Old and New Testaments. Not merely a collection of hallowed stories, the scripture underpins the theological assertions of human dignity. It marshals a cavalcade of human experiences, virtues and divine commands that elevate the understanding of man's place in the cosmos.

The deliberations and writings of the Church Fathers offer another cornerstone. Their treatises, in their rigor and spirit, breathe life into the doctrines held dear by the faithful. The epistles and exhortations of St. Augustine, the harmonious integration of Aristotelian philosophy with Christian dogma by St. Thomas Aquinas, amplify and elucidate the inherent sanctity of the human person.

Advancing through the corridors of time, we encounter ecclesiastical councils and synods, whose congregated wisdom left indelible marks upon the fabric of Catholic teaching. The fruits of the Second Vatican Council, codified in documents like "Gaudium et Spes," intricately discuss the manifold aspects of human life and dignity. These pronouncements are profound in their insight and comprehensive in their application, serving as navigational stars for contemporary issues.

The Catechism of the Catholic Church should not be overlooked. Within its pages lies a compendium of Catholic belief, drawn from scripture, tradition, and the Magisterium. The Catechism dissects and expounds upon the divine image reflected in humanity, presenting the sacred duty of moral adherence and the guiding hand of ecclesial instruction.

Encyclicals, apostolic letters, and papal bulls further articulate the teachings enshrined by the church. Works such as Pope Leo XIII's "Rerum Novarum" and Pope John Paul II's "Evangelium Vitae" delve into the social and moral obligations inherent in human dignity. These declarations resound as clarion calls to uphold justice, sanctity and the inviolable nature of life.

Among the resources, one must also reckon the various doctrinal declarations and decrees issued by the Sacred Congregations, particularly the Congregation for the Doctrine of the Faith. The writings dispersed by these offices defend, elucidate, and clarify matters of grave theological and moral import, providing authoritative guidance to the faithful.

To gain a holistic understanding, one might seek the wisdom of historical documents that predate and influence Christian doctrine. The classical works of Aristotle and the meditations of the Stoics, albeit not explicitly divine, illuminate the philosophical antecedents that dovetail with Christian anthropology and ethics.

Pragmatism is vital; therefore, contemporary publications and journals focused on moral theology and Catholic ethics ought to be perused. These publications bridge the historical teachings with modern conundrums, offering nuanced perspectives and research-based insights into enduring truths.

Lastly, there is value in studying biographies and hagiographies of saints and moral exemplars. The lived witness of these figures, whose lives were testaments to profound reverence for human dignity, provides an inspirational model for achieving the sanctity to which we are all called.

This array of documents serves as both a wellspring and a repository, enabling a profound engagement with the doctrine of human dignity. They beckon the earnest seeker to explore their depths, promising enlightenment and reinforcing the sacred nature of every human soul.